Noonan's meditations remin[...] the earliest days of life—can [...] a spiritual adventure. Drawing on her own experiences as the mother of two, Noonan illumines how God continues to "momently make" us into new beings, if we are open to it.

ANN M. GARRIDO, *Associate Professor of Homiletics, Aquinas Institute of Theology, and author of* **Mustard Seed Preaching**

Claire captures beautifully the anxiety of new motherhood, the discovery of the baby's personality and likes and dislikes, and the utter wonder and challenge of it all. We rarely have time to reflect on that kind of self-giving when we have our children. Claire has given new mothers everywhere words to describe their experience in spiritual terms and to pray through it. *Full of Grace* is a wonderful addition to a new mother's bedside table.

MARY KATHARINE DEELEY, *Director of the Christ the Teacher Institute at Sheil Catholic Center, Northwestern University, and author of* **Mothers, Lovers, Priests, Prophets, and Kings: What the Old Testament Tells Us About God and Ourselves**

Noonan draws from her own experience as well as from experts to help women move thoughtfully, mindfully, and prayerfully through the physical and emotional upheavals of pregnancy, birth, and their baby's first year. Wonderful writing and theological insights are part of the conversation, and biblical quotations are made the center of reflection. *Full of Grace* is the perfect shower gift for the new or experienced mother-to-be.

ELIZABETH JEEP, *author of Blessings and Prayers Through the Year: A Resource for School and Parish and Sweeter Than Honey: Prayers for Catechists*

Of all the ways a new mother is defined, perhaps the most consistently forgotten is that she is, along with everything else, a spiritual being. Claire Noonan's *Full of Grace* corrects this lapse with a wonderful blend of common sense and a wisdom that includes the very best of the rich religious traditions to which we are all heir. Understanding that a new mother's most precious and scarce resource is time, she offers a path to peace and refreshment that is unique and invaluable.

MARY GORDON, *author of Circling My Mother and Reading Jesus: A Writer's Encounter with the Gospels*

Motherhood is more than apple pie. It means a woman is full of grace. Grace will be yours in the reading of these essays. Your heart will be touched and your soul anointed, and you will be filled with an intuition that has found words. The intuition is grace, and the words are love.

SISTER ANN WILLITS, *retreat leader and author of the audiobook Writing Home: A Retreat with Sr. Ann Willits, O.P.*

Full of Grace

A New Year of Life
for Your Baby-and For You!

Claire Noonan

TWENTY
THIRD 23rd
PUBLICATIONS
www.23rdpublications.com

DEDICATION

To my mother, Mary Lee,
my daughters, Mary Siena
and Margaret Susan,
and to my husband, Tony,
who, in innumerable ways,
made this book possible.

TWENTY-THIRD PUBLICATIONS

1 Montauk Avenue, Suite 200, New London, CT 06320

(860) 437-3012 » (800) 321-0411 » www.23rdpublications.com

ISBN: 978-1-62785-078-0
Library of Congress Catalog Card Number: 2015946643
Printed in the U.S.A.

Contents

Paying Attention

As we enter into this new period of life called motherhood, our attention rightly and necessarily turns to our children. We truly appreciate that our lives are not our own. Some days the demands our children put on us for care and attention are so great that we cannot even manage to take a shower, let alone devote an hour to prayer. This is certainly a common experience. I was out with a friend once who asked me, "How are you?" Not the question posed as a social nicety or with a passing glance, but rather a question asked with sincere concern. Her tone gave me pause and invited a thoughtful response. Taking a moment to collect myself, much to my own astonishment, the truthful answer that emerged was, "I don't know."

So far I had gotten from my inner life that I could not even identify my own feelings when the opportunity for honest connection with a close friend presented itself. Dominican sister and preacher Janet Schlichting, OP, writes, "We wish for a soft, dark peace, a deep velvety silence, a space of soul to reflect, pray, welcome the Word." But the unavoidable reality of motherhood—especially motherhood embedded in the context of a host of other responsibilities to family, home, work, neighborhood, church—is that space and silence are rarely available. The only velvet we are likely to see is in the laundry basket! But Sr. Janet goes on: "Holding out for more focus, more peace, we are going to miss the coming…God comes to us not because we are ready, or have gotten our desires straight. God comes in Jesus, out of *ecstasis*, the overflowing love of the Trinity, with a divine desire for our healing, our salvation, and our own transformation into living Words."[1]

And so the hope for this book is that there might be another way. Not the way of velvety silences and monastic retreat from ordinary life. Nor the way of frenetic activity breeding disconnection from our inner life. But rather the way of simple attentiveness and small pauses for prayer and awareness. The hope is that as you pay attention and live with the wonder of your child—conceived, born, growing, and changing—you will begin to see yourself—also growing and changing—with the same eyes full of wonder.

In this volume, I hope to be your companion in encountering and noticing the grace of God revealed in, around, and through *you*. I hope that in entering into this sacred space, you will hear another Voice speak. And that the Voice will remind you that you are "full of grace, the Lord is with you."

CHAPTER ONE

Pregnancy and Birth

Remember the first time you saw an ultrasound? Remember the first stirring of new life that you actually felt—the quickening, as our ancestors used to say, or the "butterfly flutter," as a friend of mine described it? Remember the first kick or punch? Those movements are sure signs that this little one, though growing within you, is fully her own person.

Remember when you knew that even accounting for your tremendous determination and thoughtful preparations, in some mysterious way, his becoming happens by another power?

Sure, we stop smoking; we put down the cocktails; we take in the prescribed milligrams of folic acid. We plot out our maternity leave, decorate the nursery, maybe even open a college fund. We read and consult doctors, psychologists, educators, our mothers, our friends, our sisters. We endure some serious discomfort and inconvenience. We buy diapers and bottles, car seats and cradles, swings and blankets and rockers. Innumerable gizmos and gadgets are offered to us. We make every effort to create the right environment for growth.

By the time you make it to the moment of "meeting" your baby, the first trimester of the pregnancy is already behind you. I have heard some women say that they enjoyed pregnancy, but I have to believe they are in the minority. And sometimes I even harbor suspicions that this minority is deluded, or perhaps slightly revisionary. Maybe they were lucky. Perhaps they are just exceptionally generous and patient. If you are one of these remarkable women, hats off to you. For the rest of us, by the time we make it to this point, we've already had the unhappy experience of constant nausea (I always wondered why they call it "morning sickness" when it can literally wake you up in the middle of the night and it regularly disrupts your afternoon routines) and its embarrassing side effects (yes, there are side effects of side effects). On more than one occasion during my morning commute, I had to pull my car over to the curb to vomit in the tony Chicago suburb where I work. I felt like a drunken college student on her way home from the bars, except without the cover of darkness and the mind-numbing effects of alcohol to mitigate the shame. You have already had to excuse yourself from multiple conversations, both professional and social, to relieve the frequent urge to urinate. Which is strange, awkward, and taxing because you are so early into the pregnancy and the possibility of miscarriage is so high that you probably have not even told your coworkers or your friends that you are expecting. Your breasts are sore; you are exhausted; you feel strange cravings or aversions to food and smells. It is a bizarre experience to have your whole body changing to accommodate a person you haven't even met.

And then, at last, you lie on the examining table. The lights are dimmed; the squishy cool jelly is applied to your belly; the technician passes a wand over you. Maybe at first you see just the black and gray contrasts, perhaps a round shape or an odd angle. But in just a few seconds the wand lands in just the right place. And there she is! The amazing image of your child, so tiny, so fragile, so beautiful, and so uniquely herself.

Despite all of the discomforts and annoyances

you have endured (and you know all of that is far from over), you realize all at once that the formation of this baby is not in your control. For all of this—all of the preparations we make, all of the challenges and changes, even all of the experience of joy we take in—in the end, the growth of the baby in our wombs begins and is brought to birth by the grace of God. And we need only stay awake and pay attention. Pregnancy is a wonder to observe, to participate in, to pay attention to, but it is not—in the end—a work to be done.

MOMENTLY MAKING ME

Where were you when I founded the earth?
Tell me, if you have understanding.
Who determined its size; do you know?
Who stretched out the measuring line for it?
Into what were its pedestals sunk,
and who laid the cornerstone,
While the morning stars sang in chorus
and all the sons of God shouted for joy?
JOB 38:4–7

Truly you have formed my inmost being;
you knit me in my mother's womb.

I give you thanks that I am fearfully,
wonderfully made.
PSALM 139:13–14

And like the conception and development of new life within us, the presence and action of God in our lives is not dependent upon our readiness or our preparation—it is only the manifestation of love.

"We need only to bring our body and mind into the present moment, and we will touch what is refreshing, healing and wondrous,"[2] writes the Buddhist monk and peacemaker, Thich Nhat Hanh. During our pregnancy, sometimes the baby himself brings us into the present moment. We feel the flutter of those tiny fingers brush against us. We watch the heart pulsing rhythmically on the monitor. For a moment, we have noticed something beautiful, something beyond our plans and machinations, something outside our controls and manipulations. Something not at all unique but still truly awesome.

Just as the development of your baby in the womb is a phenomenon you witness rather than cause, so too is the work of God in your life. Your life and your development are as miraculous and inexplicable as your baby's. As the new life growing inside you comes as a precious gift, so too are you a gift. We often say it sarcastically, even caustically, to people we feel are too proud: "So you think you're God's gift?" But this is a shame, a mocking of the immensity of God's love and the power of God to create. This is not a joke or a put-down; you *are* God's gift. Your life is God's first gift to you, and you are called to make a gift of this life to the world. There is something truly amazing, literally wonder-full in this truth. If only we could notice it.

What if we were to bring the wonder that is awakened in us by the touch of our developing babies to the contemplation of our own lives? Think of it. Did you create yourself? Is the fact of your being, of your body alive, moving, stretching, resting, changing, the result of your own efforts and designs? Bring to mind the most important people in your life. How did you come to know them, to love them? What do you consider to be your greatest personal strengths or most notable talents? Likely, you have worked hard to develop, exercise, and hone them. But did you produce them? Or did they rise up in you spontaneously? Did you feel drawn to pursue them by the interior movements of your heart and mind? Isn't most everything dear to us fundamentally a gift?

Father Joseph Tetlow, SJ, a master spiritual director in the tradition of St. Ignatius of Loyola, teaches that this is a foundational insight for our whole spiritual life. The point of departure for all fruitful prayer and reflection on the present questions and concerns of my life is the initial awareness that God's majestic creative power made possible not only my birth, but is "momently making me."[3] You are being created not only in your conception, gestation, and birth, but "momently," that is, in every moment. Fr. Michael Himes writes, "God's love is given to you totally, absolutely, perfectly at every moment of your existence. If it was not, you would not be. The only reason anything exists at all is because God loves it."[4] God's gracious activity and sustaining hope within the specific context of your life "momently," in all its particularity, is a wonder to behold.

NO TWO ALIKE

My two children are now eight and three years old. And though they share the same room and hold in common many similar character traits, their birth stories could not be more different. With my firstborn, Mary, I read and planned and worried and generally tried my damnedest to orchestrate the whole affair. Once we found out we were expecting, my husband and I began to scour websites, interview friends, and consult "the experts." On the one hand, I was terrifically blessed with excellent medical care. On the other hand, I was suspicious of the American tendency to commercialize health care and to treat childbirth like an illness. On the one hand, I'd heard horror stories from friends who'd endured hours—even days—of protracted labor in the hospital setting. On the other hand, I was skeptical about all the claims to peace and tranquility I heard from the alternative health care sectors. In the end, I had taken in so many mixed messages about what to expect and what to desire that I couldn't bear to face the experience of giving birth without an expert advocate by our side. So we made plans for a "natural birth," in a hospital under the care of a doctor but with no medicinal interventions. We spent weeks looking for a doula who would accompany us through our first experience of childbirth. On the advice of a good friend, we finally settled on one woman who managed to win our trust—and as a bonus also happened to be a massage therapist!

I gave the same diligent (if slightly neurotic) attention to my professional life, in preparation for my maternity leave. I'd thought through exactly what I could accomplish in the final weeks before the baby would arrive. How would I meticulously prepare all of my papers and projects to hand off to my colleagues, and who would oversee which dimensions of my responsibilities while I was away? I consulted with my department director, my human resources office, my immediate coworkers, and my student leaders; the whole network was duly conferred with and informed. While my preparations for the arrival of the baby always made me feel a bit overwhelmed, intimidated, and undereducated, my workplace remained an arena in which I still felt competent and on top of things.

As it turned out, both my worries and my expectations were overturned by the astonishing unpredictability of birth. In the thirty-fifth week of my pregnancy, I went in for a regular, scheduled checkup with the obstetrician. Just as she was about to complete the examination and send me on my way, she had what seemed to me a stray thought: "Let me just take a look at your cervix before you go." The impromptu inspection revealed that I was several centimeters dilated and, in fact, already in labor. I'd never heard of such a thing. I had no experience of pain or hint of contractions. But my doctor sent me immediately to the hospital. I remember standing on the street corner outside of her office in the darkness and the rain, calling my husband to pick me up (I'd taken the train to the appointment), telling him that we had to go to the hospital *now*. The baby was already on her way. My husband was equally stunned. This was not a call he expected to get for several more weeks. The National Weather Service recounts that "the 4th of October was one of the largest warned severe weather events in the history of the National Weather Service in Romeoville [Illinois]. About 43 severe thunderstorm or tornado warnings were issued with almost all of them verified with hail or wind damage."[5] Metaphorically speaking, Tony and I were experiencing our own personal tornado. We were praying that the damage would be minimal.

When we arrived at the hospital, the resident examining me began to measure the contractions—increasing in frequency according to the monitoring technology but still imperceptible to the mother! Well known to the mother, due to the long-standing pain associated with a skull wedged between her ribs, but new to the medical personnel involved was the further complicating factor of a baby in breach (meaning feet down, for the novices in the group). This combination called for preparations for an emergency cesarean section. I remember telling the resident that surely she would wait to operate until my own doctor had arrived, and her answering me with a politely disguised, not to say condescending, are-you-completely-nuts-lady voice, "No, we need to move as quickly as possible." There was no time at all to wait for our carefully chosen and beautifully calming masseuse/doula.

Eventually, my doctor and my husband did join me in the operating room. And our beautiful Mary was born, safe, healthy, and tiny.

Margaret's entrance into the world was completely different. Not easily dissuaded, Tony and I decided to try again for a natural birth. We were supported in our preparations by both my doctor and our newly selected monitrice (who is essentially a doula with a nursing degree). Despite, or perhaps on account of, all of the surprises of Mary's birth, I was much less anxious the second time around. I'd let go, at least a bit, of the idea that I could plan or control this experience (though I did my best to try). One of the techniques that Tanya, our monitrice, uses with mothers to manage the pain and anxiety of childbirth is self-hypnosis. I didn't invest fully in her whole program, but with my background in spirituality the practice felt to me much like meditation. As the day of the expected delivery grew near, I began to close each day by following one of Tanya's soothing invitations to slow down my breathing, center my attention, and imagine a place of safety and beauty. In the middle of the night in my thirty-ninth week, I awoke with the pain of contraction. The previous day there had been a great snowstorm in Chicago. Through the course of the day, areas around the city experienced five to eight inches of snowfall. By the time Margaret's arrival seemed imminent and Tanya recommended the move to the hospital, the roads were clear but deserted. The night's dark edge was softened by the glistening white snow lining the streets.

There was no emergency here, but neither was there any delay. Margaret came quickly. My labor was messy and intense. None of this is appropriate for polite conversation, but even the simplest birth is a story of blood and vomit and sweat and shit. That is just the truth. I drew on the support and expertise of the whole team surrounding me. Their care and encouragement wrapped around me emotionally in the same way that the warm blankets soothed me physically. No pharmaceutical intervention was necessary. In a few short hours, Tony and I were holding our new baby girl. The tears of pain were replaced by tears of joy. The doubts about my own strength were replaced with gratitude for the grace of endurance. As one of my mom friends said: "Through childbirth I learned that I was stronger than I thought I was; I learned to trust my body. The most important thing is to have your own experience and pay attention to it."

Margaret arrived in her own way, fully her own person from the very start, already, it seemed, marking out her own place in the family. And here I was learning all over again what motherhood is and who I was becoming.

Each mother's experience of childbirth is as unique as the child being born. From natural births to cesarean sections to long-awaited phone calls from the adoption agency, premees to induced late-comers, breach to sunny-side-up, each child enters the world in his or her own way with his or her own story. For the mothers of these children as well, no two stories are the same. Each of us has her own tears of joy and pain, her own moments of fear and trust, her own experiences of loneliness and community to share. Yet, for all of us who have given birth, the story of birth is the story of our entrance into motherhood. It is the gateway into a new dimension of identity and into a new community of understanding. And if we make space for it, it is also an opportunity for new spiritual understanding, or perhaps for understanding something quite ancient all over again. For in reflective, prayerful motherhood, we are getting to know not only our children but also ourselves. In childbirth, we are meeting a new child, we are meeting ourselves, and we are meeting God.

NAMING GRACE
One of my friends made the interesting observation that when a new child arrives into our lives, we have

the privilege of naming him or her. There are so
many factors at play in selecting a name—family
heritage, religious tradition, social convention, joy
and delight. Choosing a name can be both great fun
and a great responsibility. But what we don't always
notice is that at the same time that we are naming
the baby, the baby is naming us. This person is the
first to call you "Mama." It is this child who will call
this identity out of you. It takes your child to draw
out—perhaps even to create—this part of you. We
are named not only by our parents, but also by our
children. And so, through them we meet ourselves
anew. They, in all their fragility, uniqueness, and dependence, are active participants in God's creative
plan for our lives.

In one way of reading the experience of becoming a mother, the child's development within
us and her arrival at birth can be seen as a metaphor for the whole of God's relationship with
us. Fr. Timothy Radcliffe, former Master of the
Dominican Order, makes this arresting claim in his
book *What is the Point of Being a Christian?* "God
comes to us as a child comes to a mother, in the
depth of her being, through a slow transformation
of who she is. Anything else would be violence or a
violation...We need patience because God comes to
us not as an external agent, but in the very intimacy

of our bodily being, which lives in time."[6] Through pregnancy, with childbirth, in the arrival of someone who calls us "Mama," we are transformed. We are made into someone not entirely new or different but someone more.

The spiritual and autobiographical truth that Radcliffe points out, however, is that although the entrance into motherhood is one of the most obvious transformations of our lives, it is far from the only one. It can make us attentive to the more expansive reality of God's transformational grace that is always at work within us. How might we read our history differently with this dynamic as our lens? What has the growth and arrival of your new baby been like for you? What potentialities have been called out of you already, even in these opening hours of parenthood?

And then, where before have you experienced a "becoming," a calling out of "something more" or "something new" from within you? Who else has given you a new name? What did it mean? What did it ask of you? Does the memory of the changes God has already drawn out of you give you courage and wisdom to understand what is being asked of you now?

PRAYER PRACTICE

I was fortunate to grow up in a home with very loving parents who were (and still are) deeply committed to the church. In many ways, I think my parents were exemplars in the kind of education for a life of faith that the church is aiming at when it calls all parents to be the "first heralds" of the mysteries of the faith for their children, and when it declares that "a wholesome family life can foster interior dispositions that are a genuine preparation for a living faith."[7] And yet, in some ways, I don't think I truly learned how to pray on my own, as an adult, outside of the liturgical setting, until I was in graduate theological school. Even years later, I feel indebted to my teacher, Fr. George Murphy, SJ, for giving his students a completely welcoming introduction to several different ways to pray. Since those years, I've had many more spiritual teachers who have shown me new paths to God or taken my hand as I walked more deeply down one or another. All the while, they were affirming the very sentiment that Sr. Janet expressed, the ecstatic love of the Trinity, not waiting until we've gotten it all right, but there already with a desire even greater than our own for our healing, salvation, and transformation. All of them, in their own ways, were inviting me to "see God in all things and all things in God," as the Dominican mystic Meister Eckhart famously said.

So while it is true that God is everywhere and always present to us, it is also true that we need to give ourselves the opportunity to notice, to attend to that holy Presence. While God has been in relationship with us even as we were wondrously knit in our mother's womb, as human beings we must build relationships in space and in time. There is a great range of ways in which to give structure to that space and time. We are blessed by the wisdom and generosity of our forebearers in faith who not only gave attention to God's presence in the world, but also left us a record of how they trained their eyes to see and their ears to hear. We are the heirs of millennia of prayer, reflection on prayer, and passing of experience from generation to generation. We are blessed, too, to live in the fertile and creative present where new insight and discovery of the beauty of God's life with us is emerging all of the time.

Each chapter of this book will close with one method or style of prayer. Some may already be familiar to you. You may already be quite practiced with them and know that they can serve you well as vehicles for recognizing and responding to God's gracious activity in your life. You may have met them at some early moment in life, under quite different circumstances. Perhaps they are reentering your life now simply as reminders to draw upon treasures of your past in order to embrace the possibilities of the present. Other suggestions you may be meeting for the first time. Perhaps they will be helpful new avenues by which you might encounter the presence of God at this particular time in life, a time of newness for your baby, certainly, but also for you. In any case, all are offered to you with an open hand.

Many times I have been told that there is no "right" way to pray. There are many fruitful practices that can lead us to greater awareness of the presence of God, and into deeper faithfulness to God's call to love. God is always waiting to greet us, to delight in us, and to see joy spring up in our hearts, families, and communities. The human family is characterized by great and glorious diversity. We are diverse in culture, color, intellect, humor, physique, health, gender, talent, virtue, vice, and a multitude of other qualities and characteristics. Not surprisingly, then, we are also diverse in the expression and exploration of our spiritual lives. God's tender care is merciful and intimate. God calls to us not only as a people, but also as persons. How we dispose ourselves to listen to this call will vary greatly. You are invited to take what is helpful, and to leave what distracts. All of these suggestions are given to you in the same spirit in which they were given to me. They are offered in humility, trust, and hope.

A SIMPLE MEDITATION

I was blessed during my pregnancy and in the birth of our second child to be accompanied through the changes by a monitrice who was trained in hypnosis as well as obstetrics. As part of preparing for a natural birth, in which I hoped to deliver vaginally without the use of any pain management medications, she introduced me to the practice of self-hypnosis. In her practice, this technique is used by mothers to focus their attention and concentrate their energy in order to reduce anxiety and to control the perception of pain associated with both pregnancy and childbirth. Hypnosis is used to train the mind and the body to turn attention away from the discomforts of pregnancy and painful contractions by directing them toward more soothing and relaxing visualizations. The mother or her trusted assistant selects positive encouragements, beautiful scenes, and other exercises meant to acknowledge the discomforts in the body but then minimize their effects by withdrawing the mind's attention from them. The suggestions encourage the mother's belief in her own capacity to manage the pain and even more to lovingly care for her baby.

In learning the technique, I noticed that it was very similar in many ways to various practices of meditation that I'd experienced in my theological education. For some reason this surprised me, but upon further reflection it makes perfect sense. Contemplation of the Incarnation—of the birth of Christ, God made human—teaches us nothing if not that God desires to meet us in the fullness of our humanity. As the angel of the Lord announced to Joseph, "'Look, the virgin shall conceive and bear a son, and they shall name him Emmanuel,' which means, 'God is with us'" (Mt 1:23). And John's gospel proclaims with its own poetic language, "And the Word became flesh and lived among us" (Jn 1:14). The fullness of our humanity encompasses mind, body, and spirit. It should not surprise us, then, that our minds, bodies, and spirits can all be disposed to orient us toward an encounter with the Living God. This is an ancient and global wisdom that has been obscured in the busyness of our contemporary culture. But perhaps the physical extremities of our entrance into motherhood invite us to consider a new practice. Here is an opportunity to slow down, literally take a breath, call ourselves to attention, and experience the wonderment of new life.

Before getting started, recall the words of the psalmist: *Truly you have formed my inmost being;*

you knit me in my mother's womb. I give you thanks that I am fearfully, wonderfully made." Take this verse into the meditation with you: "I give you thanks that I am fearfully, wonderfully made." You also may wish to set a gentle alarm to free yourself from any concern about keeping time. This will help to free you from any anxiety or disorientation. If you are a beginner, choose just five or seven minutes. As you read, this may feel very short, but if you are unaccustomed to the silence, it will feel like a long time. Be sure that the sound that will bring you out of the meditation is gentle and inviting, not jarring in any way. A single chime works well. If you have more experience with silent prayer, select the time that is best for you, or rely on your body's own memory to bring you out of the prayer when you are ready.

Then, find a comfortable place to sit. Place your feet flat on the floor. Rest your hands on your lap with palms up in a posture of reception, or palms down in stillness and waiting. Be at ease. Straighten your spine and lift your head without stiffening up in any way. Feel your chest opening up to receive the fullness of breath.

Now, notice your breath. Close your eyes and relax your face. Inhale slowly and deliberately. You notice that as you become more comfortable, you begin to breath more naturally, taking a deep breath that expands your abdomen rather than your upper chest. Exhale through your mouth, pushing the stresses and anxieties out. Your out-breath is a release, a letting go. Take at least ten deep breaths. Feel your body begin to relax.

Then, in your imagination, begin to move down a staircase. As you walk slowly and deliberately down the steps, count each step, backwards from thirty. 30…29…28…as you descend, with each step you become more and more deeply relaxed and at ease. 27…26…25…continue your breathing. 24…23…22…inhale the goodness of the breath of God. 21…20…19…exhale all disturbances and worries…3…2…1.

The bottom of the staircase opens up into a place of safety, warmth, and comfort. Imagine the place where you experience the care and security of God—perhaps a sunlit beach, a green forest, or a special room from your personal history or imagination. Whatever you select, step into this space now. Sit in this sacred surrounding. Recall the wisdom of the psalm, "I give you thanks that I am fearfully, wonderfully made." Simply be in the divine Presence.

When the chime sounds, repeat the verse one final time and close your prayer. In your imagination, rise from the place of warmth and safety. Know that you carry it with you, and you can return there whenever you wish. Ascend the staircase slowly and deliberately. When you reach the top, gently open your eyes. You may wish to offer a brief prayer of thanks, in your own words, for whatever gift you received in the meditation. Amen.

CHAPTER TWO

0-3 Months

NO HANDS BUT YOURS

However dramatic or painful the experience of
childbirth, there is some truth to the cliché that
all is forgotten once the baby is actually put into
your arms and you feel the weight and warmth of
her body on yours. You smell the absolutely unique
fragrance of her newness. You are simply overcome
by her beauty. If all has gone well with the birth,
soon she will stretch her neck out to you, searching
for your breast. You know from all of your reading
that your milk has not yet come in. Here is another
physical manifestation of the baby's power to create
something new in you. It is her suck that will bring
the milk out of you. But in these first few hours,
you are just becoming acquainted, and nursing

is creating connection even more than delivering nourishment.

Mostly, the baby sleeps, nestled in your arms or her father's. She is so quiet and still, curled up tightly. Unaccustomed to the open spaces of her new home in the world, she draws her knees to her chest, rests her bottom on her heels, holds her hands to her head, and sleeps and sleeps. With her right there on your shoulder, you nearly hold your breath so as not to disturb her. Once in a while, she stretches her hands and fingers out. They seem so long, so delicate, so new and yet so strangely mature. They reach out as if to say, "Here I am. I have arrived." With literally her whole life ahead of her, she is, at the same time, fully herself. It brings to mind a line from Mary Oliver's poem "What is the Greatest Gift?" The poet answers the title question:

> That you have a soul—your own,
>   no one else's—that
> I wonder about more than I wonder
>   about my own.[8]

That is the feeling—absolute wonder and the realization that this is a new person with a soul that will ever be a source of awe evoking the spiritual gift promised in the Holy Spirit. The ineffability of the love that this wonder signifies brings you to tears.

Perhaps you are blessed too by the excitement and delight of your extended family and community. They come to your bedside to welcome this little one into the world of human relationship and to refresh their own sense of wonder. Waves of gift-bearing visitors arrive to greet and admire the baby. Grandparents beam with pride; girlfriends sneak in your favorite Thai food; a bouquet of flowers arrives from the office; the siblings literally jump for joy at the sight of the brother they've been waiting to see for so long. The well-wishers cannot wait to have their chances to embrace the innocence, hope, and possibility of new life. Like the Magi at the first Noel, the arrival of these admirers confirms a new mother's feeling that the birth of her baby is truly an inbreaking of God's grace.

The presence of the larger community also acknowledges the transformation of your identity. You are recognized in motherhood as a bearer of God's grace. Literally, you have given birth to God's unique and holy blessing in the world. And despite your worn countenance, you too are marvelous to behold. Love and joy abound in hearts near to bursting.

But, of course, love is costly. The marvel and wonder is flesh and blood—and milk and tears and even poop. No matter how beautiful the card you will send to announce this little one's arrival, regardless of how flawlessly we stage the portraits of these first days destined to adorn our dressers, desks, and mantles, the truth is that love is messy. And you know now as perhaps you have never known before that love is not a feeling. It is a decision, a chosen way of being. As theologian Carter Heyward wrote, "Love, like truth and beauty, is concrete. Love is not fundamentally a sweet feeling; not at heart, a matter of sentiment, attachment or being 'drawn toward'.… Love is a choice—not simply, or necessarily, a rational choice, but rather a willingness to be present to others without pretense or guile."[9] This last resonated with me so deeply. It is difficult to muster up much pretense when you are frozen in place by the lingering effects of anesthesia and dependent on the care of an efficient nursing staff to relieve yourself. The love demanded of you in motherhood is nothing if not concrete.

A few weeks premature, Mary had great trouble learning to nurse. At first, she had difficulty latching on properly. With great compassion, our nurses and the hospital's lactation specialist visited us, offering guidance and advice. But we just couldn't seem to make quite the right connection. Before I knew it, my nipples had been rubbed raw. They were so tender they were starting to bleed. On top of that, Mary was just so small and she tired so quickly that she did not have the stamina to get enough to eat. She would fall asleep before she'd taken enough milk to nourish her growth. All babies lose weight in the first few days after they are born, but hers was dropping too quickly. And being so small to begin with, her weight loss was endangering her health. We were advised that she would have to be fed every two hours—even if that meant waking her up. Of course, waking her up meant waking me up too. Although I refused to abandon nursing altogether, we had to start supplementing with formula. Because it is difficult to tell how much a breast-fed baby is eating, we also had to record her output. We had a chart documenting the time of every wet or dirty diaper.

I was exhausted, and my husband, Tony, was advised (warned might be an even better word) to watch that my emotional spirit did not start to sink right along with my physical stamina. Many women suffer deeply from postpartum depression, but even barring that extreme, the demands of this new identity are taxing. Responding to the call of "mama" takes a toll. I began to bounce back and forth between the utterly astounding beauty of the newborn lying beside me and the overwhelming demands such a tiny creature was making on my body. It is surprising how quickly the exhaustion gives way to tears. The tears can signal muddled thinking as surely as they can symbolize joy. I desperately wanted to keep Mary by my side, but finally the nurses convinced us that they should take her to the nursery for a few hours so that I could get some sleep.

I am sure that, whatever the circumstances of your baby's arrival into the world, you also have a story of the cost of love. My sister's first babies were twins who spent weeks in the neonatal intensive care unit. The separation and worry that she endured were great strains upon her spirit. One of my dear friends had a daughter who ingested some meconium during delivery. The baby was whisked away after birth for medical care. It had already been a long, protracted, and painful labor. Although she was surrounded by caring friends, there was an essential aloneness about the experience, which was a great sorrow for her. Even in the best of circumstances, with a completely healthy baby and an experienced mother, there is no avoiding the exhaustion of labor, the blood of delivery, and the tenderness of swollen breasts.

St. Teresa of Ávila famously said, "Christ has no body but yours/No hands, no feet on earth but yours." The work of love is given to you to do. As a parent of a newborn, you feel acutely the weight of responsibility, the utter dependence of the newborn baby upon your care. You know and you learn again that being the hands of Christ in the world is not as enchanting as it sounds.

Think of the work Jesus actually did during his lifetime. Think of the bloodied knuckles of the carpenter's son who handled sharp tools and dry wood. Imagine the fishermen's companion who grabbed hold of the heavy nets and smelled of fish. Recall that he took the hand of the woman with the fever and the man suffering from leprosy, and he anointed the blind man's eyes with mud. Remember that, in the end, his hands were pierced with nails. Sometimes we can sanitize the image of Christ—all power and glory, not much muck and mire. We might equate his kindness with fine breeding or good manners. But his love was true, earthy, and real.

Jesus' faithful response to God's call in his life meant both the gathering of the beloved for great feasts and the exchange of beautiful gifts *and* the painful labor of care for people in need. If we are faithful to our call, then we should expect that, as it was with him, so it will be for us. Now called "mother," we have embarked on a magnificent journey. Saying yes to the call of love in our lives, we learn in the first few days that our "hands" too will be raw and bloody. Christian philosopher Mary Jo Leddy writes, "We must listen for the calls that summon us out of our self-centeredness."[10] Undoubtedly, the cry of the newborn baby is such a summons.

AT THE LIMIT

In a few hours, or a few days, if all has gone well, you and your baby are ready to go home. There is a comfort in being released from the constant noise, blinking lights, incessant opening and closing of doors, poking and prodding of nurses, tests and monitors, never-quite-comfortable feeling of being in bed all day, and room-temperature, grayish institutional food. Yes, I was happy to be going home. But, at the same time, the prospect of caring for this precious, fragile being who was at once my greatest love and also a complete stranger was nothing short of terrifying. The prospect of leaving the hospital was cause for both relief and anxiety.

As you leave the hospital, you are not permitted to walk by the power of your own two feet. Instead, you are pushed to the exit in a wheelchair. There is a care and tenderness to this. (Though I am sure the driver of the policy is minimizing litigation.) But the wheelchair also echoed and reinforced a nagging feeling of helplessness that sat in the pit of my stomach. There was a way in which the utter dependency of the baby underscored my own dependency, fear of inadequacy, and uncertainty.

The limitations of all my capacities were already showing themselves and I hadn't even gotten her home yet. My body had been stretched—literally—to its limit in birth. I was tender, aching, and sore all over. I left the hospital with an ice pack on my vagina and salve on my breasts. I was a wreck. My emotions, too, were stretched to their limits—from ecstatic joy to absolute exhaustion. It was incredible, really, how far I had traveled in the course of just forty-eight hours, and rarely having even left my bed.

Arising out of this utterly unique constellation of emotional, physical, and psychological strains were questions that were also deeply spiritual. How do I do this? Will I do it right? What if I fail her? For my part, my worries basically redounded to logistics and understanding. I felt I just didn't know what to *do*. Years later, a friend would share her very similar worries. She put it this way: "Other things in life you can choose what you're good at, but not this. You just have to take it as it comes." So far, "as it comes" had really knocked me for a loop.

I have learned that the experience of fear and anxiety, concern that you "just might not have it in you to be mother," is widely shared. For lots of moms, the fear manifests as worries about competence or information, like it did for me. Other mothers doubt their character. In her endearingly self-deprecating book *Operating Instructions*, writer and single mother Anne LaMott confesses, "It occurs to me over and over that I am much too self-centered, cynical, eccentric, and edgy to raise a baby, especially alone."[11] Others are burdened by fears arising from circumstances that present challenges that can feel insurmountable. You may be isolated, separated from family supports by distance or grievance. Perhaps you are saddled with financial constraints, with debt or unemployment or an income that cannot sustain your family. You may have a physical disability—your own or your child's. All kinds of things, both real and imagined, can cause fear and self-doubt. We are especially vulnerable to these spiritual prowlers when we are so worn down by the physical strain of childbirth and the sleeplessness of early parenthood.

These doubts and worries can signal the presence of the kind of fear that is decisively *not* of the Spirit. Many spiritual masters point to this kind of fear as the primary opposing force to loving freedom. Spiritual maturity, they observe, is essentially the movement from fear to freedom. This is pre-

cisely because fear can prevent us from embracing
the call, the summons, that comes to us to be Christ
in the world. Jesuit theologian Dean Brackley, SJ,
puts it this way, "Peace and joy are what we were
born for. Its necessary condition is the freedom to
love. Our happiness seems to depend on how we respond to the insecurities that besiege us. In the end,
there are only two ways to deal with them: either
we grasp for idols or we live by faith."[12]

Brackley's analysis points us toward another way
to look at our insecurities. If our fears lead us quickly down a path away from the peace and joy God
desires for us, then we must look for another way.
How can we respond in faith to the rising anxiety?
A key may be to recognize the kernel of truth that
sits at the center of the pack of mounting lies that
our fears generate. The truth we have run flat into is
the truth of our limitations, essentially of our identity as creatures—not gods but daughters of God.
Within the web of doubt and fear is an invitation to
freedom, the freedom that comes in embracing our
true identity. Fr. Michael Himes writes:

> "Recognizing ourselves as creatures means that
> we have come to grips not only with the limits
> of our physical being but with the defects of
> our moral goodness. We are not creatures in the

39

abstract; we are creatures with concrete pasts,
individually and communally. And those pasts
are not histories of pure and perfect agapic love.
Frequently, they are dark and sometimes brutal
tales of selfishness and hatred and deep despair.
And so we must accept the fact that we are all,
in one way or another, morally tarnished. That
is not to be regarded as an embarrassing or
unfortunate flaw. It must be turned into what
Augustine saw it could be, an occasion of joyful
acceptance of our dependence upon God for
forgiveness as well as existence."[13]

Although motherhood calls us to "agapic love" (that
is, love that is given entirely for the good of the other), our physical wounds and emotional worries remind us that our capacities and our histories are
far from perfect. There have been and will be many
failures to love. If love calls for "compassion, kindness, humility, meekness, and patience" (Colossians
3:12), as it most certainly does, who cannot recall
innumerable disappointments—both delivered and
received? In the most fundamental ways, we are as
dependent upon the gracious mercy of God as our
babies are. We are limited.

Here, in our limitation, lies a most amazing
and unexpected gift. Growth into freedom con-

sists first in the recognition of limitation as an opportunity for grace. The completely disarming wisdom of Christian faith overturns the cultural mythology of fierce independence in which we have been schooled. Our limitations, embraced as expressions of our createdness, of our relationship to the Creator, can be occasions of joy. They release us from the pressure of keeping up the mirage of self-sufficiency. They allow us to meet others with patience, mercy, humility, and non-possessiveness. They free us to accept the losses and disappointments that are the inevitable stuff of life. Jan Pilarski is the mother of three sons. Her youngest, Chris, lives with autism. Jan was invited to respond to Fr. Himes' claims about limits, dependence, and joy. She wrote:

> "Limits have the potential to be transformative;
> not to turn the bad into good, but providing us
> the space to discover our dependence on God
> and where our true security rests...Although
> I am learning to realize more and more what
> little control I have over my life in the large
> sense, I see my life stretching out before me
> as a prayer in which I am called to simply say,
> 'May everything be what it is.'"[14]

BEHOLD

With both of my girls, at about the fourth week of life we really started to turn a corner. By that time we'd certainly figured out the feeding situation. Mary had figured out how to latch on properly and we were comfortable now alternating between breastfeeding and the bottle. She'd begun to gain weight, and we were out of the really scary time. Margaret had been a dream since the beginning. Her birth was so much easier, and she would even sleep on her own quite well. In Mary's case, Tony had already returned to work. So she and I had to figure out a rhythm to our days. I was up to walking now, and we still had plenty of visitors. Margaret, born in late January, gave me permission to cozy up on the couch for long winter naps.

The real magic, however, was watching them grow and develop, more and more fully able to engage. At the end of the first month, the first smiles broke across their gorgeous little faces. I remember one of my dear old friends, a family physician, remarking that cuteness is a baby's only defense mechanism. It rang true for me these weeks. No matter how frustrated or tired I got, that little girl's smile brought me back to the wonder of her first moments of life.

At the end of the second month, their capacity for play emerged. Margaret "found" her first toy. At last I could rattle the rattles and shake the shakers to some effect. She could express her delight in the sound and the motion. Mary turned eight weeks right about the beginning of Advent. The all-Christmas radio stations got going. We unpacked the Christmas boxes and dug our own holiday music out of the CD tower. She seemed to love singing and dancing. A favorite of ours was *Handel's Messiah: A Soulful Celebration.* She liked Dianne Reeves and Tramaine Hawkins the best. I'd sing and we'd dance around the kitchen. She couldn't quite laugh, but her smiles were more and more animated.

At eleven weeks, Mary could bring her hands together. Purposeful action was now within her realm of ability. It is an enormous and astounding leap, actually. Margaret's independent personality was starting to emerge. She could lay under her Gymini for almost thirty minutes, playing on her own. She would laugh and smile, swatting at the toys hanging overhead, kicking her feet this way and that. It was astounding to be able to just watch her entertaining herself. There is a tremendous grace that comes in just letting "everything be as it is." What an incredible gift just to be able to watch her be herself, her playful, happy self, for a few moments.

BE STILL

This incredible development in capacity for delight, play, and recognition is such a consolation for a new mother. But engagement with a newborn is, to say the least, not all fun and games. For in these weeks, the growing alertness also means that the baby is sleeping less frequently. And just as she is beginning to express her happiness, she also expresses her dissatisfaction. The squeaks and cries easily mollified by breast or bottle give way to what sounds—to the anxious mother at least—like deafening roars of discontent. And perhaps the most maddening thing is that many times, the source of discomfort is impossible to find. You are doing your best to care and comfort, but you just cannot seem to figure out what is wrong. Or what is missing.

I remember one night in Mary's life in particular. We had family visiting us from Iowa. About 10:00 at night, after everyone in the house had gone to sleep, she woke up crying. And crying and crying. We tried all of the usual things first—feeding, changing, walking, singing, rocking. We tried bouncing, laying down, standing up, swinging, feeding again. But nothing would console her. She just kept crying and screaming. And then, for no reason I could explain, she did finally stop, just stop. She quieted down, settled into my arms, and after a while fell asleep. I never could determine what was wrong. Her ease seemed to come of its own accord. As far as I could see, it did not arrive as a result of any of my efforts or even from hers. The mood simply changed. And then she was at rest, tranquil. Whatever care or agitation had afflicted her seemed to just vanish.

My parents remember a similar night they'd had with me when I was about this age. But they had a gut-wrenching punchline to their story. In the morning, when they changed my diaper, they discovered that one of my diaper pins had come undone and was sticking into my leg. Obviously, I'd been crying with hurt, trying to alert them to the painful accident that had befallen me. They felt terribly guilty, of course. But still, there must have been a comfort in knowing what was wrong, a consolation in the explanation itself despite the silent indictment they felt at the discovery.

For much of Mary's infancy, I couldn't decipher her desires or find the cause of her grief. Perhaps because no cause was apparent, it seemed possible to me that there was no cause at all. Sometimes I surmised that the cause—whatever it might have been—was out of all proportion with the response. The only explanation I could come up with was that whatever the initial trigger for her tears, she'd worked herself up into such a tizzy that there simply was no consoling her. She wanted—desperately wanted—but even she didn't any longer know *what* she wanted. What could be done for such a one? I never could really reconcile myself to this. My mother kept telling me, "Claire, babies cry." But that wasn't an explanation or a solution.

I didn't like it, but I think my mother was right. Sometimes there is nothing to be done. The only thing to do is to be present and to be patient and to wait for the tears and the wailing to at last subside. Always, after some time, the "at last" would arrive. Her crying would slow down. The tears would dry up. And then I could cradle her, admire her, and delight in her again.

If I can give myself space enough to be honest, I realize that I am not so different from this inconsolable infant. There are many things that I worry needlessly about. There are things that start as the slightest concerns that have been worked up in my imagination to worries of epic proportions.

This confession led to me to wonder about the reason for God's pleading with us: "Be still, and know that I am God" (Psalm 46:10). "Be still." Nothing more than that. Whatever the cause of our agitation and unrest, just be still. There is nothing beyond the reach of God. The psalmist imagines the greatest catastrophes:

God is our refuge and strength,
     a very present help in trouble.
Therefore we will not fear, though the earth
should change,
though the mountains shake
     in the heart of the sea;
though its waters roar and foam,
though the mountains tremble with its tumult.
PSALM 46:1–3

Yet the call to stillness is a help and a consolation even for the minor anxieties, when even the most trivial worries cause us to fret. We are invited to respond with trust to the faithfulness of God even and especially when we cannot even identify the cause of our consternation.

"God is our refuge." No performance necessary. No test of skills or aptitudes. No expectation of success or achievement. Simply be still. What I begged of my newborn daughter, God also asked of me. "Be still. Let us just be together with nothing to distract or separate us. There is nothing more that you need. Underneath it all, what is the cause of all of your fuss and commotions? All the yearning and striving? Can you not simply let go? Do you not already have all you need? I am God, and I am here. Can you simply be still, and notice? That which you most deeply desire is already yours."

AN EVEN SIMPLER MEDITATION

During these first weeks the baby's needs are so great, and your own resources seem to wax and wane. You have been given the advice at every turn to "sleep when the baby sleeps." But I just couldn't figure out how to make that work. There always seemed to be so much to do. Mary hated to be put down, so it was difficult for me to get even any physical space apart from her, let alone time, especially after my husband returned to work. Margaret slept better on her own, but I often felt like I should be "doing something" productive while she was asleep. The dirty dishes denounced me from the sink. The thoughtful congratulatory gifts from friends continued to arrive, and the blank thank-you notes accused me from the desk. In some of the earliest days, just getting up, showering, and getting dressed was the very most I could manage. My sister-in-law said she forced herself to at least get her makeup on every day. It made her feel human, she said.

When even the simplest tasks feel overwhelmingly difficult, it is hard to fathom that there might be time for prayer. But, if possible, see if you can allow God's invitation to stillness to make at least as strong an impression on you as do the dirty dishes. Can you put your spirit before your kitchen? Give yourself the permission to acknowledge your limits, let God be God, and feel your own humanity. Allow for the possibility that your anxieties are a bit overblown, that all that you are fretting over is really not as important as it appears to be. Offer yourself the grace of five minutes of restorative privacy.

Begin as you did in the previous chapter, by recalling the words of God: "Be still, and know that I am God." Take this verse into the meditation with you. If you are worried about time, remember to set a gentle alarm. If you already have a feel for the space of the silence, select the best time for you. If you are a beginner, choose just five or seven minutes. Be sure that the sound that will bring you out of the meditation is gentle and inviting, not jarring in any way. A single chime works well.

When you are ready, find a comfortable place to sit. If you have already begun to establish a regular practice of prayer, use this same place. Your body will remember this spot and begin to orient itself to mindfulness when you take your place in it. Place your feet flat on the floor. Rest your hands on your lap with palms up in a posture of reception, or palms down in stillness and waiting. Be at ease. Straighten your spine and lift your head without stiffening up in any way. Feel your chest opening up to receive the fullness of breath.

Now, notice your breath. Close your eyes and relax your face. Inhale slowly and deliberately. You notice that as you become more comfortable, you begin to breathe more naturally, taking a deep breath that expands your abdomen rather than your upper chest. Exhale through your mouth, pushing the stresses and anxieties out. Your out-breath is a release, a letting go. Take at least ten deep breaths. Feel your body begin to relax.

Then, as you continue this slow and steady breathing, repeat the words of the psalm, "Be still, and know that I am God." Be assured that God is addressing you. Whatever the state of your environment, state of mind, state of spirit, God is inviting you to these few moments of quiet. "Be still, and know that I am God." Hear those words in your heart and pause for a few moments to take them in.

Begin to enter more deeply into the stillness and the intimacy with the Creator. Feel your creature-liness in God's presence. Continue your slow and easy breath. One by one, start to drop the last word of the psalm. "Be still and know that I am." Hear the ancient name of God, the God who called to Moses from the burning bush. "Be still and know that I AM." Breathe in the power of the divine name. "Be still and know that I." Continue with this pattern until at last you close with "Be." An invitation to the eternal present, to the only time in which we can meet our God, can live our lives, can behold the extraordinary beauty of our children, and can be released from our undue anxieties. "Be."

When the chime sounds, repeat the verse one final time and close your prayer. You may wish to express some response to God's word and presence. As you return to the normalcy of the day, know that this invitation to stillness is waiting for you always. You are invited to let go of your cries, joyfully accept your limitations, and let everything simply be what it is.

CHAPTER THREE

3-6 Months

He calls his own sheep by name and leads them out. When he has brought out all his own, he goes ahead of them, and the sheep follow him because they know his voice. They will not follow a stranger, but they will run from him because they do not know the voice of strangers. JOHN 10:3–5

I KNOW THAT VOICE

In the first few weeks of your baby's life, you have felt indispensable and have been uneasy about letting him go for even a minute or two. But in truth, at that time, he was just fine, perfectly comfortable being passed on to Grandma or Auntie or even around the room at the family party.

That is, your baby is fine, but you experience

great apprehension in letting go, even for a few minutes. With my girls, I felt enamored, responsible, attached, exhausted, delighted, burdened, and buoyed all at once. I just didn't want to be separated from the baby. Both because her beauty delighted me and because her vulnerability frightened me, I could not let go of her.

Once in a while, though, the insistence of her other admirers would prevail upon me. I'd let a visiting friend hold her while we talked over coffee. Dad would take her on long walks so that I could get some sleep. Grandma absolutely would not be denied. She'd scoop even a sleeping baby right up the moment she entered the door. When I gave the newborn over, I usually felt some awkward mix of relief, joy, pride, guilt, worry, and gladness. There was inevitably a strong reaction within me. For the sake of being sociable, I tried to keep these emotions under wraps. But I know that my mother, at least, knew they were there. She also thought I was completely nuts. She was probably right.

The baby, on the other hand, was evidently unfazed by these visitors turned caretakers. She demonstrated no particular preference for me, or her father, for that matter, over other friends and relatives. She was equally content (and equally fussy, I might add) in my arms or in the arms of any member of her growing fan club. The one exception to this, when I could swoop in with the ultimate and undeniable trump card, was when she was ready for nursing. In those weeks, the singular standout characteristic separating her mother from the rest of the pack was my breast.

A strange thing happens between you and your baby when he enters the second trimester of his life. The interchangeability of adult admirers starts to fade away. Arriving in place of the baby's early contentment with any careful cradling arms is a distinct and well-articulated (as only a three-month-old baby can articulate) preference for his parents. Playing on those police department visits to our childhood elementary school, my husband calls this the "stranger danger" phenomenon. They say that infants can recognize their parents' voices even in utero. But this emerging dynamic stretches far beyond recognition. At a certain point, usually within this period of three to six months of age, the baby just wants his mommy. You are no longer one among many. You are known, particularly and meaningfully known.

This change is a marker of the baby's development and creates a shift in your relationship. There is clarity about the attachment that the baby has developed with you that can be at once terrifying and also affirming. Their dependence upon you (which you hardly thought could get any more intense) can be frightening. Their demands can reinforce all of your insecurities. How could you possibly measure up to their expectations? How could you be all that they are expecting you to be? Being set apart in this way can make you feel singular, isolated, alone. As another friend put it, "It was so hard to feel like everyone else had it figured out and I didn't."

At the same time, since this new way of relating with you coincides with the baby's growing range of expression (no longer just sleeping or crying, but now smiling, grasping, perhaps even cooing), his desire to be with you can be communicated lovingly. The exchange that takes place between you is increasingly rich and varied. There is something overwhelming about the affection your baby feels for you. As one of my mom friends observed, "I tend to be very critical of myself, but when I can see myself through their eyes, I realize that they don't care about all of my imperfections. I am just the way I am. I expected to love them, but I didn't realize how deeply they would love me."

This dynamic of recognition, affection, preference, and dependence resonates with Jesus' extended reflection on the good shepherd. The good shepherd is one of the most beloved and ancient images of

Jesus. It originates in the gospels of Luke and John. In Luke's narrative, the good shepherd is the key figure in one of Jesus' most memorable parables. "Which one of you," he asks, "having a hundred sheep and losing one of them, does not leave the ninety-nine in the wilderness and go after the one that is lost until he finds it?" (Luke 15:4). As with all his parables, Jesus' question was perplexing to its hearers. It overturns all cultural expectations because the standard shepherding practice in the time would have been to let the one go and protect the ninety-nine. When asked, "Which of you?" the group would likely have thought, "Are you kidding me? No one in his right mind would do anything that stupid!" But Jesus goes on: "When he has found it, he lays it on his shoulders and rejoices." And our religious imaginations have never been the same again.

In the Gospel of John, the passage on the good shepherd contains one of the many "I am" statements through which Jesus reveals his identity. These metaphors illustrate Jesus' relationship both to his Father and to his disciples. Taken together, they echo the great "I AM" of the Hebrew Testament. When Moses was called through God's appearance in the burning bush on Horeb to be the liberator of the enslaved Israelites, he was afraid and doubted himself. So he questioned, "If I come to the

Israelites and say to them, 'The God of our ancestors has sent me to you,' and they ask me, 'What is his name?' what shall I say to them?" God answered, "I AM WHO I AM." He said further, "Thus you shall say to the Israelites, 'I AM has sent me to you'" (Exodus 3:13–14). This name, "I AM" is the name by which the Israelites will know the Lord, and will know the authenticity of Moses' call.

Jesus places himself within the Israelites' narrative of salvation by adapting this name of the Lord to his own life of sonship. "I am the vine." "I am the way, and the truth, and the life." "I am the bread of life." "I am the light of the world." "I am the resurrection and the life." And, in the tenth chapter, "I am the gate," and "I am the good shepherd." All of these are names by which Jesus is known. But this last, "I am the good shepherd," turns on the theme of recognition itself. The essential, defining characteristic of the "good" shepherd is mutual recognition. The shepherd *knows* his sheep *by name.* And the sheep *know the voice* of their shepherd. Just as you see in this stage of your growing baby's development, they will not go with strangers. The sheep will follow only the one whom they recognize. In drawing upon this evocative image, Jesus speaks to one of the deepest needs of the human spirit—the desire to be *known.* These elements of recognition, voice, naming, and knowing all create a bridge for Jesus' ultimate depiction of this relationship to his disciples that comes at the Last Supper when he says, "I no longer call you slaves, but friends. You are my friends."

Consider the most treasured friendships of your life. Think back, beginning with your adolescent years when your emotional life began to complexify and the spatial proximity of classroom or neighborhood was no longer enough to sustain a friendship, as it had been in your elementary and middle school days. Call to mind the names of each of your closest, dearest friends through your maturing years and leading up to today. As you review this cast of characters, is there anything you could say about all of them? Anything that would describe every relationship truthfully, despite the obvious differences among them? I suspect there is at least one thread that runs through all of these friendships, and it is that each of these people knew you, really knew you. With some, perhaps, there was an immediate resonance between you, some special interest, shared idea, or deeply held value. With these friends you felt understood, comfortable, at ease. Explanations were unnecessary. With others on your list, maybe there was some secret divulged, some truth told, some bond of knowledge shared between you that made you known to one another in naked honesty. With these friends, safety, security, and trust were foundational. You could be vulnerable and transparent. There was no need to hide or protect yourself because you had learned that in this person's company you were liked and loved for who you really are.

Sharon Daloz Parks was a longtime faculty member and senior researcher in the Harvard Divinity School, Harvard Business School, and the Kennedy School of Government. She is perhaps best known for her work studying the faith development of young adults. She has a terrific book called *Big Questions, Worthy Dreams* in which she makes this wise assertion: "If we want to learn about the formation of a person's life, a helpful question to pose is, 'Who recognized you?' or 'Who saw you?' As human beings, we all have a need to be 'seen.'"[15] She goes on to explain the hunger of young adults for access to positive images of themselves that recognize their authentic competence and qualities without minimizing the struggle inherent in developing those competencies and turning potential into excellence.

Parks is writing, as I said, about young adults, but I think her questions are pertinent for everyone. As you look back over your life, and as you think about the relationships in which you are engaged today, who recognized you? Who sees you? The real and authentic you? The you God created with manifold gifts and talents? The you of competence and beauty? And the you who is struggling with challenges both circumstantial and self-made, struggling to live authentically, lovingly, justly? Who saw you?

And though Parks's metaphor is built on the sense of sight, and Jesus' is built on hearing, the relationships they are describing have the same quality. Our babies call out to us in these months. They want to be with someone who knows who they are, someone whose voice they recognize. We all do. This yearning is our humanity reaching out for the company of God. Jesus calls back to us with our names. He is inviting us into a friendship in which we are known for who we truly are. Our mentors, our friends, and our God call to us, and we recognize their voices. The security born of intimate knowledge frees us to discover and be ourselves.

JOY IS THE SUREST SIGN

When Margaret was six months old, my mom and dad took our family on a wonderful vacation to Kiawah Island, South Carolina. They'd experienced a bit of a windfall and had always had a dream of making a trip like this. So they rented a beautiful house, big enough for all of us, on this gorgeous island. My husband and I and our two girls, my sister and her husband and their three older children, and my brother and his wife and their baby all made the trip out to the Atlantic Ocean from our Midwestern homes for a week at the beach.

It was fantastic! The big kids had great fun jumping the waves and chasing each other across the sand. All the dads took the kids out fishing one day, and my brother cooked us a fabulous feast with the catch. Mary and her cousin loved sharing a bedroom and stayed up way past their bedtimes every night whispering and giggling together. Every night after all the kids were in bed, the adults stayed up to share a drink and some good conversation. I think it was everything my parents had been hoping for.

But my favorite memory of the trip was the Wednesday afternoon I spent with baby Margaret. That day was particularly hot, and she was so young that Tony and I didn't feel comfortable having her outside in the sun for very long. Also, it was quite windy and the sand could really kick up on the shore. So, while everyone else made their way down to the beach with umbrellas, buckets, and books in tow, I decided to stay back with the baby. We literally had nothing to do for hours on end but enjoy one another's company. Away from our normal environment, I felt no pressure to answer phone calls or e-mails, wash the dishes, or go grocery shopping. I wasn't feeling anxious or tired or stressed. (OK, maybe a little tired. At this stage, Margaret was still not sleeping through the night.) We weren't rushing to make dinner or get a bath in or fighting to get to sleep. We were simply together. And as the warm, bright sunlight poured into the family room through the glass windows, all I could do, all I needed to do, was marvel at her astonishing beauty.

Mostly, we just lay there on the floor—smiling, laughing, and giggling. We looked at picture books. She watched me build towers with her cousin's blocks. She grabbed at balls and bears and bells. We rested and snacked. The great excitement of the afternoon was that she learned to roll over. This made for a great report when Grandma returned from the beach.

The sunroom was surrounded by some beautiful trees, and at one point a brilliantly red cardinal alighted on a branch right beside the window. The bird's vivid color caught my eye. For quite some time we watched him standing there, twitching his head, and letting out a chirp now and again. To this day, I cannot say for certain whether or not Margaret really saw him. Perhaps a pediatrician could help with this question, but I am not sure how far into the distance a baby can see at that age. Whatever

physical limitations were at play, the presence of the
bird with us felt like a heavenly blessing, a signal
of this day's importance. The cardinal stands in my
memory like a flag or a bookmark, reminding me to
stop, take in the beauty, and experience the delight
of my children's company. This was an afternoon
of utter delight. The uncomplicated happiness in
those tickles and smiles was, for me, the very best
that I hope for in family life.

Often, probably most often, I expend an extraordinary amount of energy trying to make my family
and myself happy—being sure that we have a clean
house and good food, that we maintain our friendships and are responsible to our communities. But
the danger and temptation for me is to spend all
my time in preparation while forgetting to embrace
the time together with full, easy, loving attention to
the person. I forget the wisdom of wasting time and
miss the experience of sheer delight.

Not surprisingly, there can be a similar dynamic
playing out in my spiritual life. The "to do" lists can
crowd out the simple delight of being in the company of God. And my high expectations and serious
demeanor can divert my attentiveness to God's delight. The thought of simply wasting time with God
can seem either unattainable or absurd. I forget the
wisdom of the sage: "Joy is the surest sign of the pres-

ence of God." But if I can allow the identity of God as Abba, of Jesus as friend, to really penetrate my imagination, then the space for delight opens up.

The prophet Hosea tells the story of the people of Israel rejecting the Lord, but in the face of such rejection the Lord says, "I was to them like those who lift infants to their cheeks" (Hosea 11:4). It is a striking image, isn't it? So intimate. So endearing. So delightful. Imagine this is God reminding you of who you are in God's sight. As you lift your baby to your cheek, how do you feel? Don't you just want to squeeze her up and give her a million kisses? Don't that little button nose and those bright eyes fill you with delight? How does it feel, in the light of your own experience as mother, to take in the prophet's metaphor? God as parent. God raising you up like an infant to her cheek. As Anthony de Mello says, "Look at God looking at you…and smiling."

Marilynne Robinson captures this essence of our relationship to God in her beautiful novel *Gilead*. The novel's lead character, a grandfather and a Midwestern pastor, writes to his grandson, "[Your mother] has watched every moment of your life, almost, and she loves you as God does, to the marrow of your bones. So that is the honouring of the child. You see how it is godlike to love the being of someone. Your existence is a delight to us…I could never thank God sufficiently for the splendor He has hidden from the world—your mother excepted, of course—and revealed to me in your sweetly ordinary face."[16] *Your sweetly ordinary face.* Do you know your own face as ordinary and sweet? As you delight in the being of your child, can you also delight in the being of God? What will be your red bird in the tree, reminding you of the joy in wasting time together?

A PRAYER TO KNOW AND BE KNOWN

Ignatius of Loyola, the sixteenth-century saint and founder of the Society of Jesus (the Jesuits), gave the church one of its great spiritual treasures—a manual of prayer entitled *Spiritual Exercises*. Developed out of Ignatius' own experience of prayer, his attentiveness to the movement of God's grace in his life, and his work with others as a spiritual director, the *Exercises* outline a four-week retreat that disposes the retreatant to make an important decision. Within the *Exercises*, Ignatius records his classic prayer, the examen. He considered this the most important prayer of a spiritually healthy life and intended that it be used not only within the retreat but in fact everyday. It is a ritual touchstone with the Lord, "a privileged moment of that 'dancing with God' in which we seek to discover where God is leading."[17] Ignatius left us this tool for creating friendship with God, for making space in our lives to be known—honestly looking at and speaking of the reality of our daily lives but always through the loving eyes of Christ, who delights in our being. The examen weaves together in beautiful simplicity Ignatius' crucial spiritual insights regarding self-examination, interiority, active service, and conversion to Christ. In five concise steps, Ignatius invites the exercitant to gratitude, holy desire, soul-searching honesty, the experience of God's mercy, and the resolution to loving service. Like a married couple lying next to one another in bed at the end of the day, exchanging stories and affections, resolving any lingering disputes, shoring up their love and commitment, the examen is a dialogue of real life. It is the place of building friendship over the long haul with the Lord in all the specificity and particularity of our lives. It is a ritual reminder that, of course, true friendship can only abide in the truth of our lived experience.

I first began to use the examen with regularity when Mary was about this stage in life, after the dizzying newness of birth and homecoming were behind us and the first signs of her personality were beginning to emerge. At this stage my body had recovered, but her fragility still required near-total

attention. I found that the stillness and regularity
of nursing gave an opening in the day for prayer
such as this. Both the baby and I were relaxed and
quiet, with nowhere else to go, nothing else to do.
We'd settled into a comfortable rhythm, and it no
longer felt impossible to give this time to prayer.
Conveniently, the fifteen to thirty minutes recommended for the examen is just the same span of
time Mary would be nursing. What a gift!

Ignatius invites us to speak to the Lord "in the
way one friend speaks to another."[18] Traditionally,
the prayer comes at the end of the day, as a review
of the day. But I found that at night I was too exhausted to be really attentive and introspective.
And also, by that time, my husband had returned
from work, and in later years my older daughter
had returned from school. So I couldn't really be
alone, quiet, and awake in the evening hours. The
mornings worked best for me, and I used that setting to review the previous day in the friendship
of God. Try to identify the time that is most fruitful for you. Although praying through the examen
even once or twice can yield insight, the key to this
prayer practice is repetition and watching the development of your friendship with God through
the passage of time. Knowing one another takes
time. Try to choose a time and place to begin that

gives you the best chance for extending an experiment into a regular practice.

Begin in gratitude. Simply thank God for the gift the day has been. Bring the disposition of gratitude to your day, and give thanks for the goodness you encountered in the course of the day. Be specific and real. Remember the card you received from a friend, the hot dish from the neighbor, the beautiful snowfall, the feel of your legs stretching out for a long walk with the stroller, the amazement you felt at the baby's latest learning. Whatever they might be, take a few moments to remember the gifts of the day and offer an expression of gratitude to God in your own words.

Situating ourselves in the disposition of gratitude is so important both for coming to know ourselves truthfully and for coming to recognize the loving voice of God speaking in our lives. It affirms the foundational principle of Ignatius' spirituality, that we are created to praise and serve God and that spiritual wisdom resides in recognizing what helps us to fulfill our purpose, and what distracts us from this purpose. Beginning prayer in praise and in recognizing the good gifts of our lives trains us in authentic self-knowledge and deepens our relationship to the God who delights in our being.

Ask for the enlightenment of the Spirit. Grounded in thankfulness, ask God that in this time of prayer you might be able to "put on the mind of Christ," that is, that you might be able to see the events, the emotions, the relationships, the demands, the gifts of your day through the eyes of Christ. As we reflect on our experience prayerfully, our guide is the Good Shepherd, not the stranger or thief at the gate.

Walk through the memory of the day with the Lord. What have you experienced in the last day? What interactions, relationships, emotions, encounters, frustrations, and joys do you notice? You might make this journey systematically, hour by hour, retracing the steps of the day until something particularly catches your attention. Or an insight might arise spontaneously—an exchange with your spouse, a reaction to the baby, a moment of elation, or a quick outburst of anger. Watch for any invitation to love that God seemed to be offering you through the course of the day. Did you accept or reject the invitation? See if any singular event stands out, calling for your deeper attention. What does it reveal about your openness to the presence and the voice of the Lord in your life? Over time, you may notice patterns emerging—fears that arise with regularity, tranquility in certain contexts, a sense of the presence of God mediated by particular persons. In honesty, humility, and trust, acknowledge the realities of your experience—internal and external—before God.

Have a conversation. Take what you have noticed into conversation with the Lord. Speak to the Lord about what you have discovered. Whatever sorrow or regret may be welling up in you, give it over to God's mercy and forgiveness. Whatever joy or gratitude, know that God shares in your delight. Whatever need or desire has appeared, ask for the wisdom to interpret its meaning. Listen for the voice of the Lord responding to your honest revelations. Be open to the surprises, the consolations, and the wisdom of the Lord.

Look toward tomorrow. As you close your prayer, with confidence ask for forgiveness for whatever ways you may have missed the invitations to love that were extended to you. Make a commitment to cultivate a new alertness to these invitations and the inner freedom to say "yes" to them in the new day. Pray for the grace to recognize the voice of the Good Shepherd in the new day and for the courage to follow the call wherever it may lead.

CHAPTER FOUR

6-9 Months

Perhaps you are lucky enough to be one of those deeply enviable women with a baby who sleeps well. If so, congratulations. I am doing my best not to hate you. You might want to skip ahead a bit. For the rest of us, these are the months in which true exhaustion sets in. About eight months after Margaret was born, we were over at my mom and dad's for a visit. My dad remarked with concern, "You look tired. Are you tired?" And it dawned on me, *Yes, yes, I am tired.* I am tired, and it makes perfect sense that I should be. I have not had a decent night's sleep in a *year*. This time last year, I was moving into the third trimester of pregnancy and starting to be too big and uncomfortable to sleep well. Also, the baby was taking up so much space inside my body that she was constantly pushing on my bladder. So that even if I could actually get comfortable, I'd be waking up multiple times each night to go to the bathroom. Then she was born, and between her nursing and her sociability, she'd never slept more than seven consecutive hours. Frequently, it was more like five or six.

At about eight months, we thought we'd nearly licked Margaret's habit of waking up at regular intervals throughout the night. We had several days in a row with her sleeping from 7:00 PM until 3:00 AM. I thought, "Not bad. I can handle this." Tony and I actually started having a glass of wine together once we had Mary settled in. We could afford to stay awake visiting, catching up with each other until the indulgent hour of 10 PM, if we knew we'd have five solid hours of rest after that. But then Margaret got hit with what we thought was a cold virus. (This is another story, but later we found out that she actually had a number of allergies that present very similarly to a cold—including the baby's fan favorites: cow's milk and applesauce.) The poor little thing could hardly breathe. Her nose was running constantly. She was just so incredibly uncomfortable, and I think she felt the worst when she was lying down. The "cold" lingered for two weeks. By the end of it, she was back to waking up two or even three times a night. And I was completely undone by the thought that soon we could be entering into the teething months, when her sleep would be disrupted even further.

Like writer Anne LaMott, "I'm crazy tired. I feel as stressed out by exhaustion as someone who spent time in Vietnam."[19] For a few days, Margaret was waking up every other hour. I just couldn't see myself using the "let her cry it out" remedy that my parents, siblings, and very brave friends kept recommending. Margaret was such a good sleeper when she was a newborn that I never thought it would take this long to get a full night's sleep. But here I was, just eight months along on this path of new life and not sure how I could possibly take one more step. Tony shared my exhaustion, and our relationship was suffering too. Our recreational life had severely diminished.

At this point, the exhaustion was not only physical but also depleting my spirit. It led to sadness and discouragement. The connection between lack of sleep and discouraged spirit is nothing unique to me, of course. Nor is it limited to new motherhood. "Nothing can sap an interest in life like chronic tiredness," wrote Roberta Bondi, recounting the wisdom of the monastic desert mothers and fathers of Christianity's early centuries.[20] Bondi draws a straight line between the lived experience of the desert monastics and the spiritual perils of modern parenthood, offering this diagnosis: "[A mother and father] may not have taken their need for breaks from the baby seriously enough to do something about it. If the need for leisure is the source of the problem, many people aggravate their acedia by filling spare time with more and more activities that do not give rest."[21]

I found that I had been guilty of this very thing. During our days together, the moment Margaret would fall asleep in my arms, I would try to lay her down for a nap as soon as I could. I always seemed to have something else I was desperately trying to accomplish before she woke up. The days of long aimless walks pushing the stroller through the neighborhood were behind us. The quiet winter naps, snuggled up on the couch for hours at a time, were no more. The idea of leisure or even of rest felt far too self-indulgent. I felt pressed to keep the house clean, the meals prepared, phone calls returned, etc., etc. Of course, by this time I had long since returned to work. So keeping up with the demands of the office weighed on me as well. And Mary, now five years old, deserved her fair share of attention. If Margaret was asleep, Mary and I had a little time to read books or play a game or talk about something of interest to her. And though I felt as if I was pushing myself constantly, I always seemed to come up short. The cumulative effect of the lack of sleep and constant activity led to a point of exhaustion and discouragement.

Discourage. Courage. What does it actually mean to be courageous, full of courage? In many ways, I think the patriarchal, individualist assumptions of our culture have co-opted this ancient Christian virtue. Now, most of our imaginings about courage have to do with men in either military uniforms or superhero tights. Often, there is a singularly spectacular rescue of a woman in danger and distress at the center of our tales of courage. But the wisdom tradition of Christian faith imagines courage differently. For the medieval theologian and philosopher Thomas Aquinas, "courage was more typically endurance. It was hanging in there, faithfully and patiently when it is hard."[22] St. Thomas calls us back to the root of the virtue, *cor*, Latin for "heart." To be courageous means to take heart, to have heart.

And what if we are losing heart? What can be done? I am reminded of the beautiful prayer of the Taizé community in the ecumenical monastery in the south of France that has created music that is beloved around the world. One piece, written for the community by composer Jacques Bethier, contains the verse, "Wait for the Lord, whose day is near. Wait for the Lord; be strong, take heart!"[23] In the style of Taizé, the verse is repeated over and over in communal song in the midst of a candlelit chapel. As I am swept up in the beauty of the harmonies, I find faith, patience, heart, perhaps even courage, returning to me. Could it be that we find our strength and heart by waiting? Can it be that in the quiet rather than in productive activity we reconnect to the Lord's energy and strength? Embellished with captivating music, the brothers of Taizé bring forward the ancient wisdom of the desert sages: "Find a time and a place to be quiet. Allow breathing time every day. Do not let prayer be replaced by frantic activity."[24] Our hearts cannot be restored with the ever more frenetic increase in the pace of our activity. Nor by a retreat from the real demands of love that entrance into motherhood makes on us. "Amma Syncletia wrote, 'If you are living in a monastic community, do not go to another place: it will do you a great deal of harm. If a bird abandons the eggs she has been sitting on, she prevents them from hatching, and in the same way the monk or nun will grow cold and their faith will perish if they go around from one place to another.'"[25] Somehow, courage is both exercised and refreshed by staying with our little hatchlings and waiting patiently enough to catch a glimpse of God.

One day, in the midst of these weeks of sleepless nights and pressurized days, something prompted me to "wait for the Lord." I was nursing Margaret on a Saturday afternoon and she fell asleep in my arms. Instead of moving her to her bed and rushing on to the next chore, on this occasion I just held her and watched her for a while. As I looked at her resting countenance, I was absolutely overcome by her beauty. I didn't have words to express the wonder and amazement I felt at the sight of her lying at peace in my arms. I simply wept. And perhaps the tears emerged, in part, from exhaustion. But as they flowed I could feel a return of courage, the restoration of heart to the work of motherhood.

LEARNING TO CRAWL

In this same period, Margaret also managed one of the most remarkable achievements of the baby's first year—she learned to crawl! It was incredible, really, watching her experiments with motion over these few weeks. Once she'd learned to roll over and back, she started testing out her weight in other ways. One of my friends at work sent me the link to a video[26] that condenses this learning process into just about two and a half minutes. It is amazingly beautiful to watch this baby (not to mention your own) engage in the incredible experiment in balance, touch, ambition, determination, rest, exploration, self-aware-ness, self-care, and curiosity that is required in learn-ing to crawl. Margaret first began scooting around the room. Then she figured out how to get her little tush up into the air but didn't quite get the idea of getting her knees underneath herself. She used her toes to propel herself forward for a while—several days at least, perhaps even a few weeks.

Somehow, in the midst of this learning process, she scratched her knee. This minor mishap led to a remarkable little quirk in Margaret's develop-ment. It must have been painful for her to put her weight on that scratched knee. And so she devel-oped her own unique method of getting across the room. Instead of the normal knee-hand-knee-hand motion that most other babies teach themselves at this stage, Margaret created her own knee-hand-toe-hand sequence. She would move forward on her left knee but alternate it with her right toe in order to protect her injured right knee. She figured out how to move without putting weight on her hurt-ing knee. She got around quite well this way and in fact never learned to crawl in the usual manner. Very quickly thereafter, she started to pull herself up onto her feet. It would be a couple of months still before she was able to stand steadily, and further on until she could walk. But during these weeks she showed her tenacity, and she impressed me with her spirited determination.

I also couldn't help but notice how remarkably adept she was at protecting herself. She'd managed with such creativity to keep moving forward despite the disruption her little injury caused. She kept progressing, kept learning, kept moving forward—literally. She wasn't going to let the cut on her knee impede her progress, but neither was she going to endure unnecessary pain. She found a way to grow adaptively. The dynamic relationship between growth and adaptation, challenge and self-care, is not the exclusive domain of childhood. These are dynamics that we have to discern and negotiate throughout our lives. They are spiritual and moral questions as much as they are physical and intellectual. How do we manage change, and not only change but growth? And what do we do when the growth we are invited to will be painful?

The reality is that most change is uncomfortable, perhaps even painful. Sociologists and organizational psychologists tell us that leading groups through times of change can be dangerous work for a leader because the group generally will try to expel the leader rather than make the change. Wise spiritual advisors and prophetic religious and moral voices know that the same dynamic operates in the interior life. When we begin to expect something great from God, and from ourselves, then change is afoot. When we know that transformation is needed, a process of conversion can begin. But we should be aware from the get-go that change can be difficult. In making preparations for the blossoming of our deepest hopes, we are accompanied by God, but conversion also awakens the forces of the status quo.

In St. Ignatius' recorded experience of his own conversion, there are two sections entitled "the discernment of spirits" wherein he described the interior movements at work in us, which are especially acute in periods of change and growth. Dean Brackley, SJ, summarizes Ignatius' vision this way:

> Ignatius presupposes that we live in a kind
> of double force-field. Human beings, their
> relationships, and their institutions exhibit two
> kinds of tendencies: movement toward light,
> truth, freedom, love, and life; and movement
> in the opposite direction toward darkness, lies,
> slavery, egoism, and death.[27]

When we start moving with purpose in the first direction, the opposite force is awakened, intent on impeding our progress. Change is not easy. Ignatius

calls this phenomenon "desolation." In times of conversion, when we are learning to crawl, we are going to fail many, many times. We may even sustain
an injury. As Ignatius puts it, for people advancing
in spiritual maturity, "it is characteristic of the evil
spirit to cause gnawing anxiety, to sadden, to set
up obstacles. In this way the enemy unsettles these
persons by false reasons aimed at preventing their
progress. The enemy discourages, stirring up fear
and sadness over the cost of perseverance."[28] Have
you ever tried of change in some way and met this
kind of resistance from within?

The Dominican mystic Meister Eckhart said,
"Whatever God does, the first outburst is always
compassion." And Ignatius writes that in times of
change it is characteristic of "the good spirit to stir
up courage and strength, consolations, tears, inspi-
rations and tranquility."[29] In many ways, I saw the
signs of courage, strength, and inspiration in my
daughters as they learned to crawl. They had the
intuitive wisdom to extend the gift of compassion
to themselves in a time of dramatic and challenging
change. Their example pushes me to attend to similar stirrings of the Spirit in my own heart.

In the processes of spiritual-life change I've
undergone, I have noticed three vehicles through
which the Spirit communicates compassion, in-

spiration, and consolation to me. Without them, I am not sure I would have been able to muster the courage to grow in truth, freedom, and love. These essential elements are imagination, community, and practice. These three supports have made it possible for me to do something differently, something new, something outside my "comfort zone," as my students would say.

Dorothy Day once wrote this about the movement of faith and justice that she founded:

> "What is it all about—the Catholic Worker movement? It is, in a way, a school, a work camp, to which large-hearted, socially conscious young people come to find their vocations. After some months or years, they know most definitely what they want to do with their lives. Some go into medicine, nursing, law, teaching, farming, writing and publishing.
>
> They learn not only to love, with compassion, but overcome fear, that dangerous emotion that precipitates violence. They may go on feeling fear, but they know what it means, they have grown in faith, to overcome it."[30]

I venture to say that the young people who came to the Catholic Worker communities came, first of all, because the very existence of the communities stirred their imaginations. From a distance, they saw that the Worker provided some example of what life could be. The aura of possibility attracted them, called them in to take a closer look. Remember the video of the baby learning to crawl? You can see in the learning process something bubbling within her. Notice that the progress from lying still to crawling is incremental. Each small "step" gives rise to the notion that the next might be possible. "Hmmm," you can almost hear her thinking, "if I can do this, I wonder if I could do that?" And then a new movement comes. A stretch in another direction, a toe planted in a new spot. I have heard many parents say that their younger children learned to crawl and walk more quickly than the firstborn because they wanted to keep up with their older siblings. The swift movements of the older children inspired the younger ones and planted in their imaginations the possibility of something better. The example of another who has done something or become someone to which we aspire nurtures hope, truth, and courage inside of us. Their examples debunk all of the fears that hold us back. A vibrant imagination holds our fears in check, quieting all of the voices of nay-saying that stir up inside of us when we contemplate or resolve to make the changes to which God invites us. So, how do we fill our imaginations with examples of gospel freedom? Who are the exemplars of compassionate living that we look to as providing the possibilities for our own lives? What are the stories we tell ourselves about what could be? Who are our "elder siblings" in the development of virtue?

Closely allied with a vibrant imagination is the power of a supportive community. Surrounded by a community of people who value our growth and cherish virtue, the notion of change and development becomes not only possible but normal, expected. St. Catherine of Siena, writing to a friend, draws the direct connection between our need for the imaginative community and the Eucharistic table: "We who eat at this table and become like the food we eat begin to do as he does—not for our own good but for God's honor and for our neighbors' salvation. Be encouraged by the thought that this fire will give you your voice and relieve your hoarseness."[31] Spiritual director Sr. Clare Wagner makes the point that surrounding ourselves with a community of women who are our spiritual friends is particularly important. In her book *Awakening to Prayer*, she writes: "Women's spirits are nurtured by connectedness with other women...Circles of women who embrace and are empowered to relate in this manner compatible with the Spirit's fruits—peaceful, kind, self-controlled, generous and joyful—are changing themselves and the world. Like a pebble in a pond, they send out circular rings of influence."[32] Her declaration raises questions for self-examination. Who embraces me? Who empowers me? Do I experience the Spirit's gifts of peace and joy in the communities of which I am a part? Does my participation in the "circles" of relationships that absorb my time and attention nurture within me a vision of a more generous and compassionate world? Does it help to shape a more kind and loving self? What are the "points of contact" in our lives that propel us forward?

It is crucial to allow the learning arc we see our babies following to remind us that growth and development take practice—repetition, experimentation, failure, and determination. There is no smooth and flawless path forward. There are many stops and starts along the way. There is never fully—at least not in this life—the perfect and uncompromised triumph of love. Always, our lives are complex, our motivations mixed, our victories partial.

There is nothing showy or easy about the love that the gospel calls us to. Whether the change we are attempting to make is social—that our lives in community might be a truer reflection of God's reign—or personal—that our own actions might conform more and more clearly to the example of Jesus' mercy and compassion—there is nothing sexy or glamorous about the process along the way. Yet in spite of this, our strength to do the work does grow as we choose again and again to say "yes" to the opportunities that God presents to us each day. Without fanfare, we can make a habit of generosity. With practice and small steps, we meet with courage the resistances that rise up within us—until we find that courage is no longer necessary, that the just thing, the loving thing, feels like the normal thing.

How might God be calling you now to embrace Jesus' vision of peace, justice, and love, in spite of the movements of desolation that might cloud your judgment or stir up a host of fears inside? Is there anything good, any gift, you have been yearning to give for some time, but it just seems like too much effort, too far beyond your reach, or too frightening to reach for? Might this be time to try, to take even a baby step in the direction of your deeper desires?

IMAGINING OUR LIFE WITH GOD
I have suggested in this chapter that courage is a necessary virtue to cultivate in order both to sustain

our vocation as mothers as well as to make changes in other dimensions of our lives—personal or communal. Furthermore, a critical component in the development of courage is a healthy, growing, and vibrant imagination. An imagination reflective of the fullness of God's reign, of the flourishing of all of creation, is a source of encouragement as we grow and develop, building up ourselves and our communities to more fully conform to this vision.

Of course, there are many ways to feed our imaginations. And indeed this is a crucial element of prayer. Our time of communion with God gives us a perspective beyond that which we are able to manage on our own. This is an essential gift of revelation—of God's voice coming to us through the Scriptures, in the historical person of Christ Jesus, and in the ongoing reflection of the church through the centuries. In our communal, liturgical prayer we hear again and again the powerful narratives of the Scriptures with their images and narratives that captivate with beauty and wonder. There are some ways in which the repetition of those stories over the weeks and years of our lives gives these sacred stories a primacy of place in our imaginations. In hearing the saving works of God in the history of Israel, the parables of Jesus, the depictions of his healing ministry, and the witness of earliest disciples, the world takes on a particular shape for us. Our view of what is good, true, and beautiful is shaped by this hearing even while we must acknowledge the other stories and visions, counter-narratives conveyed by the political and economic structures of our culture that compete with the narratives of faith for our attention and devotion.

But there are other ways in which Scripture's power to move us has been compromised. On the one hand, these images and stories may have become so familiar that we are no longer really listening. And on the other hand, because they emerge from a historical and cultural situation so different from our own, they may no longer effectively communicate their original meaning. So there is a real need to discover other ways both of allowing the images of revelation to work within us, and of bolstering their power with allied contemporary narratives. In this chapter, I would like to offer two methods of prayer, both of which work on our imaginations.

First, perhaps we could begin where we are. In these months, and in the years to come, one of the most enjoyable ways to spend time with our babies and growing children is reading to them. Already, even at this age the experts in child development tell us that the lyricism of the written language is building their intellectual capacity, preparing them to become accomplished readers. And just as they are beginning to demonstrate the noticeable ability to focus on toys and colorful objects, the beauty of the colorful images in picture books is also nurturing the soil of their young minds. Your local library is undoubtedly urging you to read to them at least twenty minutes a day. Here is a perfect opportunity to integrate prayer—an openness to listen to the voice of God—into the normal routine of our day.

Begin by reviewing the stories that are a part of your child's library. What are the words, images, and narratives you are sharing with your baby? Ask how these poems and tales resonate with the vision of the reign of God offered by Jesus' life and teaching. I am not suggesting that you limit your repertoire to religious or biblical stories. On the contrary, recall that the original biblical stories draw their meaning precisely from their connection to the ordinary features of the lives of their hearers. And remember that the wisdom of the sacraments is in the communication of God's grace through the tangible artifacts of the earth—wheat, grapes, oil, and water. So rather than imposing some narrow understanding of "religious art" on your library, look for what is holy and sacred in the ordinary and familiar, as well in the original and creative, right at your fingertips.

Some of my favorite stories to read in this way are:

- *Mama, Do You Love Me?* by Barbara Joosse, illustrated by Barbara Lavallee

- *"More, More, More," Said the Baby* by Vera B. Williams

- *The Runaway Bunny* by Margaret Wise Brown, pictures by Clement Hurd

- *Guess How Much I Love You* by Sam McBratney, illustrated by Anita Jeram

- *Click, Clack, Moo: Cows That Type* by Doreen Cronin, illustrated by Betsy Lewin

- *Old Turtle* by Douglas Wood, illustrated by Cheng-Khee Chee

- *Horton Hatches the Egg* and *Horton Hears a Who!* by Dr. Seuss

These are a few ideas to get you started, but of course the possibilities here are practically unlimited. So select one to get started that delights and challenges you. Then, simply open and read the story slowly, contemplatively, and prayerfully. Allow the lyricism of the words to stir the creativity of your soul. Let the narrative awaken in you a sense of wonder and possibility. This is the second naiveté that, as the philosopher Paul Ricoeur says, gives us purpose and power on the other side of complicating life experience. Savor the illustrations, whose beauty is itself an encounter with the immanence of the divine. What does this story suggest about what is possible in this life—for you, for your children, for your neighbor, for your community, for the world? What "light" are you drawn to in the reading of this book? Does it draw you away from the desolation of egoism? Does it speak to you of the spirit of tranquility, compassion, and freedom that are signs of consolation whose ultimate source is God? If you take this story as speaking to you, what kind of response—a response in word or in deed—would you make back to God?

Just as bringing a prayerful disposition to imaginative works can create space for the life-giving word of God to enter our lives, so also bringing an imaginative disposition to the familiar words of Scripture can create space for a fresh word of God to catch our attention. In addition to the daily examen, which we explored in chapter three, the *Spiritual Exercises* of St. Ignatius of Loyola also contain directions for an imaginative contemplation of Scripture. The original work advises retreatants to look at several specific passages from the gospels, most especially the passion narratives, which are the central focus of the third week of the retreat. But outside of the retreat sequence, really any passage of Scripture may prove fruitful in prayer. Marrying the Ignatian example with the liturgical life of the church, you may want to begin simply by praying with the gospel of the day.[33] Wherever you choose to begin, know that one beautiful dimension of this style of prayer is that you can remain with particular texts for as long as the contemplation continues to bear fruit. The text will most certainly carry a surplus of meaning, not exhausted in a single reading but dynamic and deepening as, over time, it interacts with the realities of your unfolding life experience. So if you find, in your prayer, that your contemplation of a particular passage creates an affective reaction within you, then continue to return to the same passage, attending to those emotive signals. God is communicating something of importance to you.

Begin in a quiet place and read the passage to yourself several times. Start with the text as it is. It is likely that you are already familiar with the text, but attend to it now as if you are meeting it for the first time. Read carefully the words before you, without conflating them with another version of the story (many narratives in the gospels, for example, have strikingly distinct details when you move from Matthew to Mark to Luke to John). Read it a few times so that it becomes newly familiar in its own rich detail, carefully chosen language, and particular setting. Now, ask God to reveal its meaning for you, and in you, in this very moment. With confidence in the providence of God, continue your prayer. Let the passage come alive for you. Imagine yourself within it—which character do you identify with? Where do you see yourself? In what relation to whom? Which elements of the text engender a strong feeling in you? What details become significant? What signs of desolation or consolation do you detect? Is there a change to which you are being invited? Conclude your prayer with some word of thanks to God for whatever grace you have been given.

CHAPTER FIVE

9-12 Months

A LONG, LOVING LOOK

When Mary was very young, one of my favorite ways to spend a day with her was at the zoo.
Especially during the winter months when it was
much too cold to be outside in the Chicago winds
with a baby, a trip to the zoo was the perfect way
to spend a morning because there were so many
indoor exhibits where she was safe and warm and I
had a change of pace and scenery. Much of the time,
I would simply push her around in the stroller.
Wheeling away the hours, we traversed the campus
from apes to big cats, Africa to Australia, rain forest
to farm. Here and there, I would park the stroller off
to the side and carry her right up to the glass, point-
ing out the blue frog in the corner of the terrarium

or the brown bear asleep in the hollow tree. The site and activity of the animals made for relatively interesting, if necessarily one-sided, "conversation."

And then, at about nine or ten months of age, Mary started to "talk" back. She wasn't yet able to communicate with spoken words, of course. But I was able now to witness her attentive engagement with the beautiful creatures we'd been visiting for months. She was especially enchanted by the otters and the penguins who playfully swam right up to the glass. From her perch at my shoulder she could track their swift furry or feathery movements across the window. Her eyes followed them right to left, left to right, and back again. She lit up with delight at the bubbly elegance of their aquatic dance.

A few weeks later, she added another stop to her "highly recommended" list. Within the Brookfield Zoo's building exploring the oceans, there is an exhibit just inside the entrance that simulates a wave crashing above a coral reef. Visitors stand before and beneath a Plexiglas barrier and can actually feel the ocean spray as the wave rolls in overhead. I am sure some kids are frightened by the water's roar, but Mary just loved it. A few steps further on, there is a giant round window with a ledge wide enough to prop her little feet up on. With help, she could stand there and watch the great variety of brilliantly colored fish make their way around the tank. Like the otters and the penguins, the fish were so close she couldn't miss them. She watched their movements with tremendous interest and evident joy.

As I stood beside her then, and as I recall her radiant expression now, the call to notice and to praise is awakened within me. Her utter delight in the engagement with God's marvelous creations is an example for me of the unvarnished affection that could be at the heart of our relationship with God. I am reminded of the sage reflections of "saints and poets, maybe" (to quote playwright Thornton Wilder) who saw, appreciated, and recorded their wonder. Hear these few.

Dorothy Day, speaking of her decision to become a Catholic:

> No human creature could receive or contain so vast a flood of love and joy as I often felt after the birth of my child…With this came the need to worship, to adore.[34]

Gerard Manley Hopkins, "Hurrahing in Harvest":

> And the azurous hung hills are his world-
> wielding shoulder

> Majestic—as a stallion stalwart,
>   very-violet-sweet!—
> These things, these things were here
>   and but the beholder
> Wanting; which two when they once meet,
> The heart rears wings bold and bolder.[35]

Even John Green's decidedly agnostic character, Michael Lancaster:

> I believe the universe wants to be noticed. I
> think the universe is improbably biased toward
> consciousness, that it rewards intelligence in
> part because the universe enjoys its elegance
> being observed.[36]

Theologian Walter Burghardt defines contemplation as "a long, loving look at the real." Perhaps God is always inviting us to take a closer, deeper look at the "real." So much of life is screened out of our vision by our habits of inattention. What if we were to allow ourselves to be schooled by that wide-eyed wonder of our children? What if we were to look with a similar spirit of openness through the giant windows of our world? What unfamiliar colors, movements, or sprays might spark a light within us?

It may be useful to examine the limits of our

attention from the other direction. What keeps us from "beholding" God's creation, the "elegance" of the universe? Many afflictions of mind and spirit and various deformations of culture and society limit our vision. For a moment, though, I invite you to consider these three: social isolation, the logic of commodification, and the lure of busyness.

But who is my neighbor?
In her book about the formation of Romero House, a community of hospitality in Toronto for refugees from around the world seeking political asylum in Canada, Mary Jo Leddy writes: "The greatest problem in the world today is not so much hatred of those who are different from us but the vast ocean of indifference between us."[37] In many ways, her book is an extended meditation on the effects of indifference—the ruinous effects of systemic, bureaucratic violence on her refugee friends, and the insidious effects of imperialistic individualism on her North American neighbors. It is a devastating critique of the normal social organization of wealthy, First-World societies. It exposes the ways in which we have been successful in organizing ourselves into ignoring one another, particularly "others" who are different from ourselves. The decline of American social institutions of all kinds is so well-document-

ed,[38] though, that it seems in many ways we have become strangers even to those who resemble us in most ways. We have created such a high degree of emotional distance and degraded our social capital so thoroughly that many people in our society now are not meaningfully engaged in any social unit beyond their immediate household.

As a new mother, I experienced this isolation acutely. Having stopped working to be home with Mary, I lost my life's primary avenue of adult relationship (outside my marriage, of course). Tied to her schedule of sleeping and eating, I had limited opportunity for planned social engagements. There were a few friendly faces on my block, but before Mary was born I'd never really taken the time to invest energy in my neighborhood. So I didn't really *know* anyone. I remember more than one occasion when I waited desperately—practically standing at the threshold of the door—for Tony to return from work just to have some adult conversation.

If the kind of delight that our young children experience in discovering the world is rare for us, perhaps it is because we have made our "worlds" so small. Think of the lawyer, the priest, and the Levite in Jesus' parable of the good Samaritan. They had so severely narrowed their line of sight, so sharply constricted their understanding of "neighbor," that they deprived themselves of the gift of life. Sometimes we view the main action of the parable as the Samaritan saving the life of the man left for dead by the side of the road, but the question that Jesus was actually responding to was the lawyer's. "Teacher, what must I do to inherit eternal life?" (Luke 10:25). In recognizing the man in distress as his neighbor, the Samaritan was neighbor himself. To use the language of the sociologist, neighborliness is the way we build bridges of social capital. Our communal ties are mutually enriching. The Samaritan is an example to the lawyer: "Go and do likewise."

Have we, like the priest and the Levite, similarly stripped our lives of unfamiliar colors and textures? Have we walked with indifference past the suffering of others? And in so doing, have we made ourselves into strangers? Could our babies be calling us to a transformation akin to the one Jesus invited the lawyer to consider? What if we were to lift up our eyes beyond the current boundaries we walk within? What if we were to gaze through new windows? Imagine new relationships? What life-giving opportunities might be awaiting us?

Maximum return
There is a long-standing tradition within the Christian churches critiquing industrial capital-

ism. It gained prominence, especially, with the publication of Pope Leo XIII's encyclical *Rerum Novarum* in 1891. At the moment, Pope Francis is probably the world's number one spokesperson for this message. These men are joined by hosts of other Catholic, mainline Protestant, and evangelical leaders, activists, and ordinary people who decry the dehumanizing effects of widening global wealth gaps, the demise of organized labor, and the "throwaway culture" that reduces human beings to instruments of production or engines of consumption. These are crucially important messages that deserve attention, study, and response—especially in the spirit of neighborliness that the gospels proclaim. But within the context of considering an invitation to the practice of contemplation, I would like to entertain a slightly different analysis of the impact our economic life has had on middle-class North Americans. This insight is put forth and developed by theologian Vincent Miller in his book *Consuming Religion: Christian Faith and Practice in a Consumer Culture*.

The argument is complex and multifaceted, and it builds up to a compelling depiction of Christianity in the postmodern age. At the beginning of the book, Miller sets out his purpose, clarifying that this book is written not as another in a long line of critiques of conspicuous consumption and the accumulation of wealth. Rather, his project is to analyze and assess the ways in which the dynamics of the *act* of consumption have radically altered the postmodern person's ability to relate to any faith tradition. Indeed, he claims that we fundamentally understand ourselves as consumers. This is our primary identity and self-conception. And this worldview provides the setting into which all of our relationships—familial, social, religious, and environmental—are inserted. "Commodity logic is insidious," Miller asserts. "Love is reduced to a calculus of maximum returns, relationships to an exchange of emotional commodities, persons to things. It is not a question of consciously choosing such evaluative criteria. This logic is our cultural default, the form in which we are most likely to cast our deliberations. The question of why we love someone is reflexively translated into a question about what we love about them."[39]

I would like to suggest that our children have not yet been trained in this logic. Their ability to wonder and marvel at the world around them is a natural disposition that has not yet been colored by the cultural default of "commodity logic." They are not yet asking, "What can I get out of this?" They are simply able to appreciate the world as it is. (Granted, there seems to be a dramatic shift here when the terrible twos set in, but that's a reflection for another book.) Their "long, loving look" has the quality of sincere appreciation rather than an assessment of use or value. In a sense, they may be more skilled practitioners of authentic contemplation than we are. As Mary gazes through the window at the otters, the penguins, and the fish, she is not making some convoluted calculation of their worth. She is simply noticing the color, the animation, the "real" before her eyes.

Is it possible for us to unlearn the logic of commodification? Or at least to switch off the default setting? How might our relationships be transformed if we began to love one another, not love things "about" one another? What if we could turn a contemplative, loving eye—in place of the evaluative eye of the consumer—upon ourselves? Our natural environment? Our faith communities? God? What wonders might we discover with "a long, loving look at the real"?

The cult of busyness

Closely related to the insidious logic of commodification are the intense expectations of productivity that dog us. We seem to be locked in a constant pressure cooker that demands we demonstrate our value at every turn. And "value" is strangely measured in busyness. Think of the content of even your most casual exchanges at work. How often does one party respond to the other with some lament about how much he or she has to do? And watch how the cult of busyness follows you home. If we are trying to keep our professional lives and raise our children, there is a constant exhaustion in keeping all of the balls in the air. If we have chosen even a few months of maternity leave, we are often worrying if we are missed at work or how we could possibly let go of our babies when the leave is over. If we have chosen to stay home, we replace the long list of demands our work made on us with a whole new set of household expectations. Or we may be battling desperately with the loneliness of having left all of those demands and relationships behind.

Law professor, mother, and foreign policy expert Rosa Brooks says it simply: "We've created a world in which ubiquity is valued above all."[40] At some point, we have to realize that the cult of busyness is a spiritual dead end. Might our children be inviting us into a different way of understanding value? Of appreciating the world? Of recognizing our full humanity—and theirs? Truthfully, our babies are not scanning our calendars and perusing our "to do" lists to assess our worth and value. If we are observant, we see the loving looks they give to the real. Might we accept their invitation and pause to do the same?

DA, DA, DA

During the same period in which we witnessed the expansion of the girls' attentive vision, we also began to see a marked growth in their ability to communicate. The noises and babbling that had first emerged at about six months now began to take on some shape such that we could recognize the intention of meaning. Evidence of their verbal capacity was beginning to appear. We couldn't tell for sure, but at ten months we thought we could make out "Da, Da, Da" as Margaret called out to her dad. (Both of my girls, to the surprise of no one who knows their mother, turned out to be early and big talkers.)

Tony and I were not as disciplined as some of our friends about teaching them sign language, but during these months they also managed to start communicating meaningfully with their hands. At nine months, Mary could wave "bye-bye." She loved visiting the public library at story time because she could watch and attempt to mimic the librarian's motions during the sing-alongs. After months and months of parental solo performances of "The Itsy,

Bitsy Spider," "Wheels on the Bus," and the like, in these days we were at last enjoying the satisfaction of a response.

It was a great deal of fun to watch and listen to the girls experimenting with language and enjoying this newfound level of engagement in community. My mother had always maintained that parenting got a lot easier for her once her babies could talk. Many women love those early months with cuddly, sleepy infants, but she always preferred a child she could actually understand. I heartily agree. With the development of their communication skills came an expansion of mutuality in relationship with my daughters that I relished. I was astonished by how gratifying it felt for them to register some recognition of the antics I employed to entertain and amuse them. The interaction was a very welcome change to my tired Ben Stein imitation, "Bueller, Bueller?"

I could tell that the girls themselves were just as anxious to garner a new measure of recognition from me. As their facility with communication grew, so did their ability to detect adult ignorance. In short, at this age they were beginning to understand that I didn't understand. Margaret in particular got more whiny and demanding. I believe that she was trying her best to communicate and was frustrated that Tony and I were not able to read her desires. What sounded mostly like babbling to us was certainly her best effort at speech. And as we would soon learn, she had quite a mind of her own. Margaret was not one to be content with going along with the program. She had definite opinions and desires. Unlike her elder sister, pleasing others was not among her highest priorities. "Would you people get it together," she seemed to be saying with her outbursts of tears. "I need something here!"

Some days I pined for that contented baby I used to know who slept away most of the day in her bassinett. It was a challenge to remember that this too was a stage that they would soon outgrow. (With Margaret now at age three, we are just about through with the tantrums. The girl of strong opinions and high standards, though, is here to stay, I think.) But on a deeper level, it is heartening to see that the desire to connect is, in fact, itself a connection. Both the girls and I wanted to know that we were understood, and wanted so much to understand the other. In this dimension of our relationship, I hear the echoes of the Scriptures.

> O LORD, you have searched me
>   and you know me.
> You know when I sit down and when I rise up;

> you discern my thoughts from far away.
> You search out my path and my lying down,
>   and are acquainted with all my ways.
> Even before a word is on my tongue,
>   O LORD, you know it completely.

PSALM 139:1–4

The psalmist writes with what feels like utter confidence. Like the young child who has found her "voice," the song of praise reverberates with the delight of connection. The psalmist revels in the security of the relationship and the ease of communication. What a marvelous feeling to know the closeness of the Lord.

And yet, in the psalms that follow this, Psalms 140, 141, 142, and 143, there is a different affective quality altogether. The blessed assurance of Psalm 139 has all but disappeared. In its place there is a palpable sense of concern, almost alarm. The psalmist sounds not quite desperate but certainly apprehensive. The writer is frightened by the wickedness surrounding him. He cries out to the Lord for help, pleading for attention: "But my eyes are turned toward you, O God, my LORD; in you I seek refuge; do not leave me defenseless" (Psalm 141:8). Like the tears of our children who are not at all sure that we understand and will respond to them, the unreserved trust of Psalm 139 has seemingly vanished.

And yet, the relationship is not abandoned. Not unlike the wide variations of success we have in communicating with our youngest children, our relationship with God can feel alternatively astonishingly intimate and alarmingly distant. The wisdom of the Scriptures—and of motherhood—seems to be: stick with it. There is no reason to expect that either relationship will deliver a perfect communion of mind and spirit. There are, inevitably, radical swings between joyous connection and fear of abandonment. Whatever the emotion of the moment, keep showing up. Keep singing. You don't want to miss those little fingers climbing "up the spout."

ONE YOU WALK

As the old saying goes, "One you walk, two you talk." So to honor the first tentative steps of our little ones, and taking a cue from the ways in which their ability to engage their surroundings and express their appreciation has grown so dramatically during these months, I offer two related methods of prayer by walking. The central insight shaping each of these methods concerns the relationship between the body's sensual capacities and the spirit's inner journey. Each affirms "the real" of human life in God that is both material and spiritual. In each, we engage the senses—especially touch, sight, sound, and smell—to deepen our awareness of the created world, including our own selves. And we trust that the embodied engagement with creation is truthfully a means through which God is communicating with us.

Walk a Labyrinth

A labyrinth is a single concentric circle path found in religious traditions throughout the world and dating back thousands of years. Although it resembles a maze, the labyrinth is not a puzzle, a game, or a trap. There is only one path that winds into the center of the circle, and back out again. There are no dead ends, and it is impossible to be lost within it. It is a spiritual tool that invites its visitors to physically engage the metaphor of path, journey, pilgrimage, procession, and centering by walking mindfully. The most famous is probably in Chartres Cathedral in France. Set within the stone floor during the Middle Ages, the Chartres labyrinth was used by the Christian faithful of the time as a substitute for making a pilgrimage to Jerusalem. In recent decades, many churches, retreat centers, and schools have built labyrinths, and they are often open and available to the public. Labyrinth enthusiasts have created a vibrant online network, including many

sites that help pilgrims find a labyrinth near their
homes. Handheld labyrinths have also been created
to simulate the movement of pilgrimage for those
who, for whatever reason, cannot access a walking
path.

Once you find a labyrinth accessible to you, it
may be helpful to follow a simple pattern as you
use it. Often, labyrinth pilgrims find their movement progresses in three stages: let go, receive insight, and return.

At the entrance to the path, pause and bring
yourself into the awareness that you are already and
always in the presence of the Source of All Being.
Let go of whatever cares or concerns distract you
from the center and source of all life. As you allow
your mind to settle into quietude, walk toward the
center. Receive the unique graces of each step along
the way.

At the center of the labyrinth, pause once again.
Feel the ground beneath your feet and the currents
of air around you. Is there an insight you are being
offered? An energy for living you are being invited
to receive? A grounding, centering Presence you can
feel? Remain at the center as long as you wish.

As you move back along the path, out from the
center and back into ordinary time, cherish the gift
you have received. Ask how this awareness or in-

sight may be woven into the fabric of your daily life. Be assured that whatever the path, the ground is always God. How can you respond now to the "real" of your life with this deep knowledge?

I Set Before You…

The second invitation to prayer is a very simple one: namely, just to go for a walk. A walk around the block or through the neighborhood, a hike in the woods or down a path by the lake. Be on your own or push a napping baby. Simply walk. But walk contemplatively. That is, as you walk, take a "long, loving look at the real." On this short journey to some destination or none, what do you notice along the way? What do you see? Hear? Smell? What can you feel? What is set before you?

As you walk, allow the word of the Lord to set the context for your noticings:

> The word is very near to you; it is in your
> mouth and in your heart for you to observe.
> See, I have set before you today life and
> prosperity, death and adversity…I have set
> before you life and death, blessings and curses.
> Choose life so that you and your descendants
> may live. DEUTERONOMY 30:14–15, 19

When you return home, record your observations. What did you notice as you walked? What captivated your attention? What sight or sound, sensation or smell, lingers with you? Spend some time journaling about what you have experienced. Reflect on the dynamics of life and prosperity, death and adversity, that may be at work within you and around you. What did you behold? What have you observed that gives rise to praise and wonder? What lament comes to your lips? What stirred a desire for conversion or change? What plea for help and assistance needs to be heard? What "hurrah" do you wish to express?

CONCLUSION

At the beginning of this new year of life, you were offered the invitation to give yourself the gift of time and space to be attentive not only to the development of your baby but to the dynamics of your own interior life. In some ways, the notion was very simple and straightforward: for a few moments—perhaps as little as five minutes each day—just be still and notice the presence of God's grace in your daily life. Likely, the invitation is more easily offered than accepted, simpler in word than in deed. So many distractions compete for our attention, demons of busyness and isolation dog us, and petty fears and powerful social expectations afflict us. Truthfully, even noticing and naming these unhealthy movements afoot is a gift of God's enlightening vision. But I hope that there has been much more in this time for you.

As you take stock of this year, I hope you will find that it has indeed been—that *you* have indeed been—"full of grace." For the Lord most certainly has been with you. The transformation your baby has undergone these months is nothing short of wondrous. This is more than evident. But you too have changed and grown, learned and developed. You have new insights and experiences, new capacities and responsibilities, new dimensions of identity and understandings of self, new wisdom and priorities, and new stories and memories.

Your prayer—as well as your daily experience— has shaped you. And if you continue to allow for the luxurious necessity of prayerful attention, its blessings will deepen. Returning even to the memories of this special year will nourish your spirit for years to come. Give yourself some space now for prayerful recollection of these months.

What was your red bird in a tree? What playful otter swimming past the window stirred you with delight? Who called to you in the loving voice of the Good Shepherd? When did you feel the life-giving effects of the good Samaritan's neighborly love? What wisdom did you receive in the labyrinth?

In her prayer, which was at once deeply mystical and entirely practical, St. Catherine of Siena heard the Lord telling her, "Here is the way, if you would come to perfect knowledge and enjoyment of me, eternal Life: Never leave the knowledge of yourself.

Then, put down as you are in the valley of humility you will know me in yourself, and from this knowledge you will draw all that you need."[41] We too would do well to accept this invitation, to follow this way. In the long, loving look at the real, we find all we need to share in the joy and the life of God.

Notes

1   Janet Schlichting, "Advent-Christmas: The Education of Desire,"
    Word and World vol. 27, no. 4 (Fall 2007), 392-393.

2   Thich Nhat Hanh, *Living Buddha, Living Christ*
    (New York: Penguin, 2007), 24.

3   Joseph A. Tetlow, *Choosing Christ in the World* (St. Louis:
    The Institute of Jesuit Sources, 1989), 201.

4   Michael J. Himes, *Doing the Truth in Love* (New
    York: Paulist Press, 1995), 103.

5   National Weather Service, available from www.crh.noaa.gov/
    lot/?n+2006_ord_summary; Internet; accessed December 1, 2014.

6   Timothy Radcliffe, OP, *What is the Point of Being a
    Christian?* (New York: Burns and Oates, 2005), 78.

7   *Catechism of the Catholic Church*, #2225.

8   Mary Oliver, "The Greatest Gift," in *Red Bird* (Boston: Beacon, 2008), 76.

9   Carter Heyward, *Our Passion for Justice: Images of Power, Sexuality,
    and Liberation* (New York: The Pilgrim Press, 1984), 272.

10 Mary Jo Leddy, *The Other Face of God* (Maryknoll, NY: Orbis, 2011), 67.

11 Anne LaMott, *Operating Instructions* (New York: Anchor Books, 2005), 4.

12 Dean Brackley, *The Call to Discernment in Troubled Times* (New York:
    Crossroad, 2004), 18.

13 Himes, 32.

14 Himes, 36-37.

15 Sharon Daloz Parks, *Big Questions, Worthy Dreams:
    Mentoring Young Adults in Their Search for Meaning, Purpose,
    and Faith* (San Francisco: Jossey-Bass, 2000), 128.

16 Marilynne Robinson, *Gilead* (New York: Picador, 2006), 52.

17   Brackley, 251.

18   Ignatius of Loyola, *Spiritual Exercises* in *Ignatius of Loyola: Spiritual Exercises and Selected Works*, trans. by George E. Ganss, S.J. (New York: Paulist Press, 1991), #54.

19   LaMott, 20.

20   Roberta Bondi, *To Love as God Loves* (Philadelphia: Fortress, 1987), 75.

21   Ibid.

22   Radcliffe, 75.

23   A choral arrangement of the song can be heard on the website of the music publisher GIA available from http://www.giamusic.com/search_details.cfm?title_id=8084&vr=true ; Internet; accessed February 14, 2015.

24   Bondi, 75.

25   Radcliffe, 77.

26   Irene Lyon, "Crawling—Feldenkrais with Baby Liv" available from https://www.youtube.com/watch?v=14gWirURq6I; Internet; accessed February 8, 2015.

27   Brackley, 46.

28   Ignatius, #315.

29   Ibid.

30   Dorothy Day as quoted in Paul Elie, *The Life You Save May Be Your Own: An American Pilgrimage* (New York: Macmillan, 2003), 438.

31   Catherine of Siena, "Letter 6, to Fr. Bartolomeo Dominici" in *The Letters of St. Catherine of Siena: Volume I*, trans. by Suzanne Noffke, O.P. (Binghamton, NY: Medieval and Renaissance Texts and Studies, 1988), 50.

32   Clare Wagner, *Awakening to Prayer: A Woman's Perspective* (Cincinnati, OH: St. Anthony Messenger Press, 2009), 63.

33   The U.S. bishops of both the Roman Catholic and Episcopal churches post the readings of the day on their websites: usccb.org and espicopalchurch.org/lectionary, respectively.

34   Dorothy Day, *The Long Loneliness* (San Francisco: Harper and Row, 1981), 139.

35   Gerard Manley Hopkins, "Hurrahing in Harvest," in *Poems of Gerard Manley Hopkins*, ed. Robert Bridges (Digireads.com, 2010), 27.

36   John Green, *The Fault in Our Stars* (New York: Dutton, 2012), 223.

37   Leddy, 95.

38   See, for example, Robert D. Putnam, *Bowling Alone: The Collapse and Revival of American Community* (New York: Simon & Schuster, 2000).

39   Vincent Miller, *Consuming Religion: Christian Faith and Practice in a Consumer Culture* (New York: Continuum, 2005), 37.

40   Rosa Brooks, "Recline, don't 'Lean In' (Why I hate Sheryl Sandberg)," in *The Washington Post,* February 25, 2014 available at http://www.washingtonpost.com/blogs/she-the-people/wp/2014/02/25/recline-dont-lean-in-why-i-hate-sheryl-sandberg; accessed March 14, 2015.

41   St. Catherine of Siena, *The Dialogue.*